CW00546843

# SHORT CUTS

INTRODUCTIONS TO FILM STUDIES

## OTHER SELECT TITLES IN THE SHORT CUTS SERIES

THE HORROR GENRE: FROM BEELZEBUB TO BLAIR WITCH  Paul Wells
THE STAR SYSTEM: HOLLYWOOD'S PRODUCTION OF POPULAR IDENTITIES  Paul McDonald
SCIENCE FICTION CINEMA: FROM OUTERSPACE TO CYBERSPACE  Geoff King and Tanya Krzywinska
EARLY SOVIET CINEMA: INNOVATION, IDEOLOGY AND PROPAGANDA  David Gillespie
READING HOLLYWOOD: SPACES AND MEANINGS IN AMERICAN FILM  Deborah Thomas
DISASTER MOVIES: THE CINEMA OF CATASTROPHE  Stephen Keane
THE WESTERN GENRE: FROM LORDSBURG TO BIG WHISKEY  John Saunders
PSYCHOANALYSIS AND CINEMA: THE PLAY OF SHADOWS  Vicky Lebeau
COSTUME AND CINEMA: DRESS CODES IN POPULAR FILM  Sarah Street
MISE-EN-SCÈNE: FILM STYLE AND INTERPRETATION  John Gibbs
NEW CHINESE CINEMA: CHALLENGING REPRESENTATIONS  Sheila Cornelius with Ian Haydn Smith
ANIMATION: GENRE AND AUTHORSHIP  Paul Wells
WOMEN'S CINEMA: THE CONTESTED SCREEN  Alison Butler
BRITISH SOCIAL REALISM: FROM DOCUMENTARY TO BRIT GRIT  Samantha Lay
FILM EDITING: THE ART OF THE EXPRESSIVE  Valerie Orpen
AVANT-GARDE FILM: FORMS, THEMES AND PASSIONS  Michael O'Pray
PRODUCTION DESIGN: ARCHITECTS OF THE SCREEN  Jane Barnwell
NEW GERMAN CINEMA: IMAGES OF A GENERATION  Julia Knight
EARLY CINEMA: FROM FACTORY GATE TO DREAM FACTORY  Simon Popple and Joe Kember
MUSIC IN FILM: SOUNDTRACKS AND SYNERGY  Pauline Reay
MELODRAMA: GENRE, STYLE, SENSIBILITY  John Mercer and Martin Shingler
FEMINIST FILM STUDIES: WRITING THE WOMAN INTO CINEMA  Janet McCabe
FILM PERFORMANCE: FROM ACHIEVEMENT TO APPRECIATION  Andrew Klevan
NEW DIGITAL CINEMA: REINVENTING THE MOVING IMAGE  Holly Willis
THE MUSICAL: RACE, GENDER AND PERFORMANCE  Susan Smith
TEEN MOVIES: AMERICAN YOUTH ON SCREEN  Timothy Shary
FILM NOIR: FROM BERLIN TO SIN CITY  Mark Bould
DOCUMENTARY: THE MARGINS OF REALITY  Paul Ward
THE NEW HOLLYWOOD: FROM BONNIE AND CLYDE TO STAR WARS  Peter Krämer
ITALIAN NEO-REALISM: REBUILDING THE CINEMATIC CITY  Mark Shiel
WAR CINEMA: HOLLYWOOD ON THE FRONT LINE  Guy Westwell
FILM GENRE: FROM ICONOGRAPHY TO IDEOLOGY  Barry Keith Grant
ROMANTIC COMEDY: BOY MEETS GIRL MEETS GENRE  Tamar Jeffers McDonald
SPECTATORSHIP: THE POWER OF LOOKING ON  Michele Aaron
SHAKESPEARE ON FILM: SUCH THINGS THAT DREAMS ARE MADE OF  Carolyn Jess-Cooke
CRIME FILMS: INVESTIGATING THE SCENE  Kirsten Moana Thompson
THE FRENCH NEW WAVE: A NEW LOOK  Naomi Greene
CINEMA AND HISTORY: THE TELLING OF STORIES  Mike Chopra-Gant
GERMAN EXPRESSIONIST CINEMA: THE WORLD OF LIGHT AND SHADOW  Ian Roberts
FILM AND PHILOSOPHY: TAKING MOVIES SERIOUSLY  Daniel Shaw
CONTEMPORARY BRITISH CINEMA: FROM HERITAGE TO HORROR  James Leggott
RELIGION AND FILM: CINEMA AND THE RE-CREATION OF THE WORLD  S. Brent Plate
FANTASY CINEMA: IMPOSSIBLE WORLDS ON SCREEN  David Butler
FILM VIOLENCE: HISTORY, IDEOLOGY, GENRE  James Kendrick
NEW KOREAN CINEMA: BREAKING THE WAVES  Darcy Paquet
FILM AUTHORSHIP: AUTEURS AND OTHER MYTHS  C. Paul Sellors
THE VAMPIRE FILM: UNDEAD CINEMA  Jeffrey Weinstock
HERITAGE FILM: NATION, GENRE AND REPRESENTATION  Belén Vidal
QUEER CINEMA: SCHOOLGIRLS, VAMPIRES AND GAY COWBOYS  Barbara Mennel
ACTION MOVIES: THE CINEMA OF STRIKING BACK  Harvey O'Brien
BOLLYWOOD: GODS, GLAMOUR AND GOSSIP  Kush Varia
THE SPORTS FILM: GAMES PEOPLE PLAY  Bruce Babington
THE HEIST FILM: STEALING WITH STYLE  Daryl Lee
INTERNATIONAL POLITICS AND FILM: SPACE, VISON, POWER  Sean Carter & Klaus Dodds
FILM THEORY: CREATING A CINEMATIC GRAMMAR  Felicity Colman
BIO-PICS: A LIFE IN PICTURES  Ellen Cheshire
FILM PROGRAMMING: CURATING FOR CINEMAS, FESTIVALS, ARCHIVES  Peter Bosma
POSTMODERNISM AND FILM: RETHINKING HOLLYWOOD'S AESTHETICS  Catherine Constable
THE ROAD MOVIE: IN SEARCH OF MEANING  Neil Archer

# PRISON MOVIES

## CINEMA BEHIND BARS

### KEVIN KEHRWALD

**WALLFLOWER**

LONDON and NEW YORK

A Wallflower Press Book
Published by
Columbia University Press
Publishers Since 1893
New York   Chichester, West Sussex
cup.columbia.edu

Copyright © 2017 Columbia University Press
All rights reserved.
Wallflower Press® is a registered trademark of Columbia University Press.

A complete CIP record is available from the Library of Congress

ISBN 978-0-231-18114-3 (cloth : alk. paper)
ISBN 978-0-231-18115-0 (pbk. : alk. paper)
ISBN 978-0-231-85104-6 (e-book)

Columbia University Press books are printed on permanent and durable acid-free paper.

Printed in the United States of America

Cover image: *Midnight Express* (1978) © Columbia Pictures

# CONTENTS

Acknowledgements   vii

Introduction: After the Crime is Over   1

1   Prison Films of Pre-Code Hollywood: Big Houses,
Death Houses and Chain Gangs   17

2   Women's Prison Films of the 1950s and Early 1960s   44

3   Identity and Violence in Popular Prison Films from the 1960s
to the 1990s   68

Afterword: Post-9/11 Prison Movies and the Era
of Mass Incarceration   99

Bibliography   112

Index   118

# ACKNOWLEDGEMENTS

I would first like to thank Yoram Allon, Commissioning Editor at Wallflower Press, for not only encouraging this project but for shepherding me through the entire process: without your good faith, patience and generous spirit this book would not have been possible. I would also like to thank the entire staff at Wallflower Press, with a special thanks to the copy editors who do such valuable work. Thanks to Frostburg State University tech guru Brian Wilson for working his magic on the images. Thanks also to Nina Forsythe who read part of an early draft of the introduction and who is the best grammar hound I know. Thanks too to Keith Schlegel who read early chapters and whose maddeningly insightful comments pressed me to think and rethink. And rethink again. You can take that as a compliment, and then I'll take you out for a bourbon (maybe not even the cheap stuff). I also owe a huge debt of gratitude to Loocy, without whose daily protection from postal workers, cats and UPS drivers this book would not have been possible. Good girl. And to Ella, the smallest human in the house with the biggest brain. Thank you, little girl, for giving me time to write, for reminding me it's time to quit and for distracting me from time to time to make me smile. Any big ideas I lost while you were talking about *Battle of the Network Stars*, *The Golden Turkey Awards* or the Marx Brothers were well worth it. And lastly, to Kristin. Thank you so very much, love – for everything. Before I met you, I didn't even know what an Adventure Trip was. Now I have one every day.

Kevin Kehrwald
January 2017

## INTRODUCTION: AFTER THE CRIME IS OVER

'From this day on, your world will be everything that happens in this building.'

Warden in *Escape from Alcatraz*

In the opening sequence of *Escape from Alcatraz* (1979), director Don Siegel begins with a wide shot of the San Francisco Bay. The camera soon pans left and we see the city through the steel cables of the Golden Gate Bridge, a view that hints at the inevitable incarceration to come. As the camera settles in on a distant, ominous shot of Alcatraz Island, rain begins to fall and evening passes into night. We hear no music, only the ambient sounds of the bay, until a single snare drum begins playing in a methodical military cadence, making our march to captivity seem orderly and precise. We then see Frank Morris (Clint Eastwood) being accompanied down a ramp by two men in trench coats. Morris, too, is in a trench coat, unshackled, seemingly an ordinary citizen being ushered along by two companions. He is quickly given over to two men in guard uniforms who place him on board the *Warden Johnston*, the actual boat used to transfer prisoners from San Francisco to Alcatraz. Once below deck, he is manhandled and shackled, completely at the mercy of the authorities.

When Morris arrives on the island, spotlights follow his every move, high-angled shots conveying a feeling of constant surveillance. At the induction centre, he's searched, passed through a metal detector and ordered to 'strip down'. A doctor examines Morris as if he's an animal, forcing his mouth open and picking through his hair, looking for lice. We hear buzzers, footsteps and gates closing. Lightning flashes and we're suddenly transported to the cellblock where Morris will serve out his time. Again he is flanked by two men as he walks down the block. This time, however, he's completely naked and vulnerable. Morris is placed in his cell, bars slam shut, and the guard says sardonically, 'Welcome to Alcatraz.' After another flash of lightning, Morris fades into the darkness, thoroughly encased in 'The Rock'.

It is, to say the least, a captivating opening. Although we know virtually nothing about Frank Morris, audiences then, as now, knew plenty about the screen persona of Clint Eastwood. The westerns and action films of Don Siegel – *Coogan's Bluff* (1968), *Two Mules for Sister Sara* (1970) and *Dirty Harry* (1971) – and the Spaghetti Westerns of Sergio Leone – *A Fistful of Dollars* (1964), *For a Few Dollars More* (1965) and *The Good, the Bad and the Ugly* (1966) – had established Eastwood as the iconic figure of the self-reliant outsider, the powerful anti-hero who administered justice as he saw fit. In a wonderfully ironic twist, however, in *Escape from Alcatraz*, Siegel cast Eastwood not as the enforcer of the law, but as someone completely at the mercy of it.

Though the movie is set in 1962 and based on an actual escape attempt, one that still fascinates the public imagination, there is little doubt that the film resonated with the audiences of its day. A box-office success, *Escape from Alcatraz* was released on 22 June 1979, just weeks before US President Jimmy Carter delivered what was later termed by the media as his 'malaise speech'. In the Oval Office address, Carter spoke of a nation suffering a 'crisis of confidence', a pervasive belief that America's best days were behind it. Without dealing in specifics, the speech addressed a nation weary from political assassinations, Vietnam and Watergate, inflation, energy crises and long lines at the gas pumps. The situation would grow even worse just a few months later when over sixty American embassy workers were taken hostage by students in Tehran for 444 days in retaliation for providing the ousted, Western-supported Shah of Iran safe entry into the US. Rightly or wrongly, this led many to see Carter as an ineffectual, feckless leader who, in the 'malaise speech', blamed America's sober mood on Americans themselves.

Viewers of *Escape from Alcatraz* must have seen something of their real condition in the film's pensive, melancholy tone. The island is a hopeless, enclosed space, a world where resigned men stare longingly at a city in the distance, realising that their best days are behind them. As the warden's words in the epigraph that starts this introduction attest, Alcatraz is all there is, and there is no hope for a better future. Enter Clint Eastwood. Frank Morris emerges from the demoralised collective as both a visionary and a man of action. Rather than philosophising on how he came to be where he is, he begins, with steely resolve and cool rationality, to design a solution to the problem. As the *New York Times* critic wrote at the time of the film's release, *Escape from Alcatraz* is 'a first-rate action movie that is about the need and the decision to take action, as well as the action itself' (Canby 1979).

In casting Eastwood, Siegel assured that audiences would recognise Frank Morris as both 'Dirty Harry' Callahan's opposite and twin. Morris, of course, is a criminal, and Callahan a lawman. But like Callahan, who disdained a bureaucratic legal system that allowed for Miranda rights, search warrants and civil liberties at the perceived expense of natural justice, Morris disdains an oppressive prison system that has completely stripped away those very protections Callahan railed against. The warden's conservative, hardline ideology ('We don't make good citizens. We make good prisoners') is shown to be as equally oppressive as liberalism's protections because it does not allow for individual liberty.

The prison world and inhabitants of Alcatraz, then, function on many levels: as American mythology, allegory and guidebook. Audiences saw a star they associated with action, self-reliance and rugged individualism deprived of those very qualities, and then regain them. They found an effectual, optimistic leader who could find his way out of a bleak situation and, significantly, take others with him. Unlike President Carter, Frank Morris took responsibility and provided answers for the malaise of the island. Clearly, the film addressed the spirit of the times (as prison movies often do) and spoke to an audience hungry for a mythic figure who promised a better future and carried through with a plan. In a very odd way, the convicted felon, Frank Morris, tapped into the same latent desires that Ronald Reagan exploited to ascend to the presidency and replace Carter in 1980. Morris didn't promise, as Reagan's campaign slogan did, to 'Make America Great Again', but he did administer hope to a downtrodden,

Fig. 1: In a flash of lightning, Frank Morris (Clint Eastwood) becomes encased in 'The Rock'

demoralised group of souls by simply uttering a sentence Carter never did: 'I may have found a way out of here.'

Like many established genres, prison movies reveal much about the cultures out of which they arise. If it's true that you can tell a great deal about a nation by the way it treats its prisoners, it's also true that you can tell a great deal about a society by the way it portrays its prisoners on screen. Although this book focuses primarily on prison *films*, it's worth noting the sheer volume of prison-based narratives recently created and currently being produced as television series, documentaries and reality shows. The HBO drama *Oz*, for example, ran for six seasons, from 1997 to 2003, producing 56 episodes. The Netflix series *Orange is the New Black* is, at the time of writing, in its fourth season, having garnered a great deal of popular success and critical acclaim. The FOX drama *Prison Break* ran for four seasons, from 2005 to 2009; and the UK's ITV ran *Bad Girls*, set in a women's prison, for eight seasons, from 1999 to 2006. The 24-hour news channel MSNBC frequently runs lengthy weekend marathons of *Lockup*, a reality show/documentary series that profiles guards and inmates at various penal institutions around the United States, to date having produced over 230 hour-long episodes. *Lockup* also spawned the spin-offs *Lockup: Raw*, *Lockup: Extended Stay* and *Lockup: World Tour*, contributing to what *Atlantic* writer James Parker called a genre of 'prison porn' (2010). As Aurora Wallace describes, 'the reality format endeavors to provide a factual account of real-life experiences, but with the shared goal of enter-tainment' (2015: 55).

To further underscore the point of current saturation, the following is but a partial list of other documentary and reality shows offered by vari-ous networks: *60 Days In* (A&E), *Behind Bars: Rookie Year* (A&E), *Beyond Scared Straight* (A&E), *Louisiana Lockdown* (Animal Planet), *Death Row Stories* (CNN), *First Week In* (Discovery), *Women in Prison* (Investigation Discovery), *America's Hardest Prisons* (National Geographic), *Hard Time: Worst of the Worst* (National Geographic), *Jail* (Spike), *Babies Behind Bars* (TLC), *Cellblock 6: Female Lockup* (TLC) and *On Death Row* (created by Werner Herzog for Channel 4 in the UK).

Prison narratives are clearly enjoying immense popularity at the moment, but they have been present in films since the silent era. As Alison Griffiths notes, 'Both American cinema and the movement known as the "new penology" came of age between 1900 and 1920, inviting an inquiry into the fascinating ways in which they informed one another' (2012: 420). While Griffiths focuses primarily on spectatorship and the effects of non-theatrical exhibitions of films within prisons on inmates and the institu-tions themselves, she underscores the significant point that the modern prison system and the modern medium of cinema have been intertwined from their very beginnings. Laurel and Hardy, for example, mined the comic possibilities of prisons in several film shorts: *The Second Hundred Years* (1927), *The Hoose-Gow* (1929) and *Pardon Us* (1931). Stan Laurel starred on his own in two earlier films, *No Place Like Jail* (1918) and *Detained* (1924). Buster Keaton also made the comic short *Convict 13* (1920). Those early film comedies – along with a few melodramatic features, such as *Condemned!* (1929) and William Dieterle's daring *Sex in Chains* (1928) – gave way to a wave of dramatic, often tragic, pre-Code prison films of the 1930s. But it was during the Great Depression that the genre truly began to form, starting with George W. Hill's *The Big House* in 1930. Hill's film, penned by Frances Marion, established many of the norms of the prison genre and set the stage for the hundreds of prison movies to follow.

What constitutes a prison film, of course, is open to debate (and will be addressed below), but Paul Mason places the number produced at over three hundred in the last century or so (2006: 191). On his popular website, 'Prison Movies', Eric Penumbra lists over 540 prison films. Regardless of the exact number, however, the existence and popularity of so many prison narratives begs the obvious question: Why the fascination with incarceration?

Nicole Rafter argues that conventional prison movies 'are essentially fantasies, films that purport to reveal the brutal realities of incarceration while actually offering viewers escape from the miseries of daily life through adventure and heroism' (2006: 163). David Wilson and Sean O'Sullivan agree with many of Rafter's points, but suggest that regarding prison films as mere escapist fantasies 'dismisses Hollywood genre prison films as having nothing to say about prison and providing us with no information that might inform our understanding of penal issues' (2004: 90). This need for 'understanding', whether genuine or imaginary, is a primary reason for the genre's appeal, because prisons operate mostly in secret. As Michel Foucault revealed in *Discipline and Punish: The Birth of the Prison*, during the eighteenth and nineteenth centuries, the punishment of crime stopped being an open spectacle (such as torture in the public square) and became a matter of captivity behind closed doors. This more 'humane' system we know today is spread across different disciplines (medicine, psychology, social work, etc) and functions to punish even the smallest infractions through bureaucratic procedures and mandates. As Foucault describes the logic supporting the system, 'it is the certainty of being punished and not the horrifying spectacle of public punishment that must discourage crime' (1977: 9). Punishment, which was once obvious, has now become invisible to the public at large. As Paul Mason points out, 'what is particular about prison compared to other arms of the criminal justice system – the police and the courtroom, for example – is their inaccessibility, their shrouding in secrecy which negates informed public knowledge about them' (2006: 195). He notes, 'The invisibility of punishment brought about by the birth of the prison has ensured that media representations of incarceration contribute, at some level and in some way, to public knowledge and comprehension of penal culture. The hidden environs of bars, cells, stairwells and razor wire are made visible in a spectacle of punishment offered by prison narratives of the media' (2006: 191). Despite the fact that in America alone an astonishing 2.2 million citizens are incarcerated, the reality of what happens behind bars is largely unknown to the majority. To Elayne Rapping, the current crop of prison reality shows are 'resonant of earlier eras in which punishment for crime was not only physical and brutal, but also publicly visible: a ritualistic spectacle that served both as a warning and as a moral education for a public socialized to see crime in terms of evil, of unforgivable and unacceptable social transgression' (quoted in Wallace 2015: 55). The less first-hand knowledge we have about prison, the more it's mediated, and the more it's mediated, the more it serves to remind us of the consequences of crime.

A second reason for the endurance of the prison genre involves the unique bond that viewers form with the central characters. The prison genre, perhaps more than any other, creates in the viewer an intense psychological identification with the inmate protagonist, regardless of guilt. For some viewers, that identification may result from a deep-seated cultural belief in innate depravity, the notion that all people are morally corrupt from birth. If there is no such thing as innocence, the convicted, like us all, must be guilty of something, and is therefore deserving of punishment on some level. The 2016 HBO mini-series, *The Night Of* (based on the 2008 season of the BBC series *Criminal Justice*) provides a perfect example. Nasir 'Naz' Kahn (Riz Ahmed) is a seemingly ideal son, a college student and tutor who on one fateful night steals his father's taxi and indulges in alcohol, drugs and sex with a young woman. When he wakes to find the woman murdered in her bed, he flees, only to be arrested, charged with murder and placed on Rikers Island. Intuitively we know that Naz is innocent of the crime of murder, but the series underscores his guilt of capitulating to his basest desires. If he hadn't given in, he would not have found himself where he is. His failure, then, lies in being human.

Even if viewers do not hold such beliefs, identification is typically heighted through the induction scene, a process that often occurs at the very beginning of the film, as it does in *Escape from Alcatraz*. If it doesn't happen at the opening of the film, it usually happens very early on, as in *Cool Hand Luke* (1967), *Midnight Express* (1978) and *The Shawshank Redemption* (1994). Psychoanalytic theory has done much to explain the viewer's complicated relationship to images and characters on screen, but it might be more valuable to simply consider the emotional response to the witnessing of initial imprisonment. When we watch a prison movie, we place ourselves in the inmate's circumstance and wonder: What has become of me? What are the rules of this place? What will I have to do to survive? How will I get out? And who will I be if I do get out?

Only the horror genre may rival such heightened identification — for prison movies, like horror films, put viewers in extreme psychological distress. A key distinction between the two genres, however, may account for a closer identification with the inmate than the horror victim. As Carol J. Clover points out, identification in horror films (and slasher films in particular) tends to alternate between the killer and the victims. Clover notes that our identification with a single character does not really emerge until the end, when we relate to what she terms the 'Final Girl', the last surviving victim left to confront the killer. She states: 'We are linked … with the killer in the early part of the film. Our closeness to him wanes as our closeness to the Final Girl waxes… If, during the film's course, we shifted our sympathies back and forth, and dealt them over to other characters along the way, we belong in the end to the Final Girl; there is no alternative' (2002: 79). In prison movies, however, viewers identify with inmate protagonists from beginning to end. Our identification may shift occasionally from prisoner to prisoner, but we rarely identify with the slasher's equivalents, such as the sadistic guard or the sociopathic inmate. There are, in fact, very few prison films that ask viewers to identify with guards or irredeemably disturbed inmates at all, with the notable exceptions of *The Green Mile* (1999) and *Bronson* (2008), respectively. On the whole, viewers bear a far more consistent masochistic relationship to a single inmate protagonist in prison films than an alternating sadistic/ masochistic relationship to multiple characters in horror films. While watching prison films, our suffering is focused. This, coupled with the absence of the supernatural often found in horror films (*The Green Mile* again being a notable exception), intensifies our sense of realism, anxiety and dread.

This leads to a third and fundamental reason for the prison genre's endurance. At their core, prison films are about self-preservation at the hands of oppressive authority and the opportunity for personal redemption. Like history itself, prison films portray long stretches of idleness punctuated by eruptions of violence and tests of character. Such occasions, whether a simple violation of policy, a full-scale riot, or an individual act of integrity, signify moments of rebellion and liberation. As such, they are fraught with danger. Prisoners arouse empathy as they find themselves not only in terrible places, but in terrible dilemmas. Snitch and win early release, or keep quiet and serve another ten years. Affiliate with one group, become the enemy of another. Resist inhumane treatment, be sent to the hole. In this way, prison films amplify the issues we face in everyday life. They put conscience and self-interest in conflict and make us rethink our reactions to our own and others' oppression.

## Prisons, place and genre

In the broadest sense, prison movies are first and foremost about prisons, closed spaces where the legally guilty pay their presumed debts to a society that often quickly forgets them. The very existence of the prison film, however, signals an opening into the prison world. These films tell the stories of men and women at the mercy of institutional punishment, characters who are forced to survive the system's cruelties and indignities, and who often seek redemption in one form or another, be it through rehabilitation, martyrdom or freedom. Prison movies are not really about crime, though crimes may occur in them. Nor are they about criminals *per se*, though criminals certainly appear in them. And while such films tell the stories of prisoners, it is significant that the genre doesn't take its name from its principle character, such as its oft-perceived generic cousin the gangster film does. Rather, it takes its name from the institution in which the prisoner is housed. Simply put, we do not watch prisoner movies; we watch *prison* movies. The correctional system's organised administration of punishment at odds with the human desire for self-determination becomes a primary arena of thematic exploration.

Fig. 2: Typical prison movie iconography from *Riot in Cell Block 11* (1954): fences, stone walls, razor wire and guard tower.

Crucial to that exploration is setting, an element of *mise-en-scène* the prison genre emphasises more than any other. Many genres are characterised by setting, of course, such as the science fiction film, which commonly sets its stories in a fantastical future. But as David Desser notes, 'science fiction can be set literally anywhere: twenty thousand leagues under the sea, the center of the Earth, the moon, Mars, and beyond, in galaxies far, far away' (2014: 348). Its use of setting is nebulous and at variance. The prison film's setting, however, is specific, and its iconography remarkably consistent from one film to the next: towering concrete walls, rows of claustrophobic cells, barbed wire, iron bars, the warden's office, the cafeteria, the shop, perilous exercise yards, unveiled shower stalls and ominous guard towers. All of these material images are easily summoned up when thinking of a prison film.

The heightened importance of setting in the prison film can perhaps best be understood through its association with the most well-established genre of them all: the western. Despite pronounced differences, both genres take their names from the environments in which they place their characters. As Edward Buscombe points out, the setting of the West is essential to the western's thematic content. He notes that if 'you want to deal with the sense of fear, isolation, and excitement engendered by great cities, you won't do it very well within the framework of the western' (2012: 17). However, 'because of the physical setting, a western is likely to deal successfully with stories about the opposition between man and nature and about the establishment of civilization' (ibid.). In similar fashion, the enclosed world of the prison provides opportunities to tell stories about the opposition between power and oppression, and the maintenance of self. The tight quarters force characters and audiences alike to confront vexing issues of morality, as well as issues of race, class, gender and sexuality. Because there's nowhere to go, the prison space becomes something of a microcosm of society as a whole, one that forever wrestles with the fundamental human themes of tolerance, freedom, justice and mercy – and, of course, their opposites.

The audience's eager consumption and quick recognition of the prison film's generic conventions have also allowed it to remain a dynamic and culturally relevant form, qualities crucial to its endurance. As Thomas Schatz notes:

Films within a genre represent variations on a theme, so to speak; the theme itself, as a manifestation of fundamental cultural preoccupations, may remain essentially consistent, but without variation the form necessarily will stagnate. The widespread exposure of genre films to the audience and the demand that filmmakers sustain audience interest in popular forms encourage continued manipulation of generic conventions if the genre is to maintain its vitality and cultural significance. (2012: 117)

Again, much like the western, the prison film has manipulated its stock characters and conventions to remain vital and interesting to audiences over time. Where the western has the self-reliant hero, the inexperienced tenderfoot, and the civilising frontier woman, the prison film has the savvy lifer, the naïve fish and the devoted love interest. As Stephen Prince notes of the western: 'The genre's richness and complexity are evident in the diversity of ways that it may portray these character types' (2014: 254). So too with the prison film. Not all savvy lifers, for example, are made the same. Some may be benevolent teachers, as with Virgil Caine (F. Murray Abraham) in *An Innocent Man* (1989), whereas others may be inarticulate clods, as with Butch (Wallace Beery) in *The Big House* (1930). Further, prison films, like westerns, are highly malleable and able to incorporate diverse narrative forms. Just as there is western tragedy (*The Shootist*, 1976), western comedy (*Blazing Saddles*, 1974) and western musical (*Paint Your Wagon*, 1969), there is prison tragedy (*I Am a Fugitive from a Chain Gang*, 1932), prison comedy (*Stir Crazy*, 1980) and prison musical (*Jailhouse Rock*, 1957). All such films speak to different audiences, but all are recognised as operating within the bounds of the prison genre because of the place in which the characters are housed. As with any genre, prison movies give us recognisable structures and formulas while allowing for seemingly infinite innovation and variation. This also allows for the creation of sub-genres, stories that focus on chain gangs, death row, riots, reform or escapes.

The prison film's extreme reliance on setting is also something that distinguishes it from the western somewhat. One might, for example, read *Star Wars* (1977) as a western even though it does not take place in the traditional West. The forces of good and evil battle over the contested territory of the galaxy. The themes and structural elements of the prison movie, however, cannot as easily be transferred to a setting outside the prison. Although Mary Findley argues forcefully that the 'rightful place' for Rob Reiner's *Misery* (1990) is that of 'the first of [Stephen] King's prison trilogy' (2008: 91), it's not a prison movie proper because Paul Sheldon (James Caan) is not *institutionally* incarcerated. Prison movies need the bars in a way that westerns sometimes don't need the West. Lastly, whereas the western is vast and expansive, covering miles and miles of territory, the prison is small and ordered. If the western has a literary equivalent, it would be the great American epic, long and sprawling; the prison film, however, is a poem, highly distilled and condensed.

### Toward a definition

So what exactly makes a film a prison film? In determining key genre characteristics, it's helpful to invoke Rick Altman's distinction between *semantic* elements, 'common topics, shared plots, key scenes, character types, familiar objects or recognizable shots and sounds', and *syntactic* elements, 'plot structure, character relationships or image and sound montage' (1999: 89). This book will expand on both of those elements and illustrate them with examples from clearly identifiable prison films from the 1930s to the present, for as Altman states (with a slightly critical tone), 'genre critics prefer to deal with films that are clearly and ineluctably tied to the genre in question' (1999: 17). For now, a simple working definition may be useful: a film becomes a prison film when the imagery and effects of incarceration overshadow all other aspects of the film. A movie like *Riot in Cellblock 11* (1954), for example, is clearly a prison film because it takes place almost entirely within the walls of the prison. It begins with a documentary-style overview of then-recent US prison riots before settling in on its own fictionalised account of an inmate uprising. Other films set almost entirely in prison include *20,000 Years in Sing Sing* (1932), *Cool Hand Luke* and *The Longest Yard* (1974).

Screen time set within a prison, however, should not be the sole determining criterion. Many movies can be regarded as prison films even if several scenes are not set in a prison. *I Am a Fugitive from a Chain Gang*, for example, contains a great many scenes of James Allen (Paul Muni) chained to his fellow inmates in a southern prison, yet it also spends significant amounts of time chronicling Allen's attempts to survive and thrive as an

Fig. 3: A wild-eyed James Allen in the final scene of *I Am a Fugitive from a Chain Gang*.

escapee in the outside world. What qualifies it as a prison film, however, is that Allen's conviction and experience in the prison dictate every narrative event that follows. Determined to bring about his dream of becoming a civil engineer, Allen rises to prominence in his profession but lives in constant fear of being discovered. After being blackmailed into marriage, he eventually turns himself in and ends up back on the chain gang, from which he escapes again, presumably living the rest of his life on the run. In the film's famous final scene, Allen's former girlfriend, Helen, offers to give him money. When he refuses, she says, 'But you must, Jim. How do you live?' Allen utters the haunting line, 'I steal', while fading into the night. The trauma of the prison experience and the constant fear of capture leave him seemingly mad, paranoid and penniless, and his disappearance into the darkness suggests a total loss of autonomy.

Yet a character does not necessarily have to have absconded to feel the repercussions of imprisonment. Characters who serve their full sentences are also subjected to the realities of life as an ex-con. One of the effects of having been in prison is to carry the prison inside even while physically being outside. In *Jailhouse Rock*, for example, less than a third of the film takes place in a prison, yet incarceration impacts everything that happens to Vince Everette (Elvis Presley) from that point on. After serving twenty months for manslaughter for accidentally killing a man in a bar fight, Everette leaves the institution jaded and bitter. As he works to rebuild his life and become a professional singer, he has to be careful not to commit another transgression against the law, however minor, lest he be sent back to prison for violating parole. After roughing up a record producer for stealing one of his songs, Everette is confronted by his partner and love interest, Peggy, who states, 'Isn't that dangerous? I mean he might have you arrested or something.' Under correctional control, Everette is always only one violation away from being reincarcerated. Everette also has to contend with the sudden appearance of his former cellmate, Hunk Houghton, who gains release and demands Everette make good on a bogus contract he signed under false pretences. Though the film is relatively light it tone, it makes clear the point that for the convict, the present and the future are always dictated by the past.

In some cases, a movie can also be considered a prison movie without a prison appearing at all, a condition that seems to belie the point above about the essentialness of the institution. Although not prison films in their purest forms, perhaps, certain films portraying convicts on the run induce the same kinds of anxieties – often only heighted by the escape – as characters in full captivity. The bars in these films become largely metaphorical. A movie like *The Defiant Ones* (1958), for example, qualifies as a prison film even though it does not include a single scene within a prison. The film begins with inmates Noah Cullen (Sidney Poitier) and John 'Joker' Jackson (Tony Curtis), chained together, escaping from an overturned prison transport truck. The rest of the film portrays the two men trying to avoid capture. The chain itself signifies the material condition of their confinement, but even when they manage to remove the chain, they are still imprisoned by their circumstance. Though outside the walls, they never experience true freedom. In effect, the entire world becomes their prison because they are not able to move about freely within it. *The Defiant Ones* conveys the same kind of mania, tedium and claustrophobia found in films set entirely within prison walls. Cullen and Jackson are still under the influence of the penal system, and, like Paul Allen and Vince Everette, will be in one way or another for the rest of their lives.

At the risk of sounding dogmatic, denoting what makes a film a prison film requires distinguishing between films that portray incarceration through due process and films that depict mere confinement. To qualify as a prison film, the captive must have been convicted – this is the key distinction that disqualifies *Misery*. In *The Truman Show* (1998), for example, Truman Burbank (Jim Carrey) is confined to an enormous studio set, yet he is not a prisoner in the sense that he has been prosecuted, tried and condemned. This eliminates many movies featuring kidnappings, hostages and abductions, such as *Dog Day Afternoon* (1975), *Ransom* (1996) and *Room* (2015). It also excludes the majority of prisoner of war films, such as Billy Wilder's *Stalag 17* (1953) and John Sturges' *The Great Escape* (1963), since the characters are merely interned for the duration of a war rather than having been prosecuted for war crimes. (The final chapter will, however, address films that investigate the current thin line between what it means to be a detainee and prisoner.) Other types of films that may have a great deal in common with prison movies proper, yet remain outside the scope of this study, include the mental institution movie, where characters often enter voluntarily or are committed rather than convicted – such as James Mangold's *Girl, Interrupted* (1999) – and the boarding school movie, where characters are often restricted, disciplined and punished yet are students rather than convicts, such as in Lindsay Anderson's *If...* (1968). While fascinating and worthy of close examination, such films are primarily, in Altman's words, 'crossbreeds and mutants' (1999: 88). Reform school films, however, do meet the criteria if the juveniles have been sentenced by a judge to serve time in an institution for the committal of a crime, such as in the James Cagney vehicle, *The Mayor of Hell* (1933). Whether of age or a minor, what matters is the loss of liberty at the hands of the criminal justice system.

Lastly, to qualify as a prison film, the prison should be the principle subject of investigation and the dominant agent of oppression. Though Charlie Chaplin's *Modern Times* (1936) has some very memorable scenes set in prison, that institution is hardly the film's focus. Rather, the prison is presented as merely one arm of a larger capitalist system that produces mindless work, dehumanising technology and crippling poverty. The prison, the factory and the streets all operate on the same plane and become the sites of resistance through which Chaplin demonstrates the tramp's romantic insistence on compassion, play and dignity.

On a final note, a study of this size cannot possibly be comprehensive. A limited number of films are discussed in the hopes that the ideas found in them can be applied by the reader to other prison films not included in this book. Chapter one sets out to further define the genre, explore its beginnings in the Great Depression, and delineate its norms. Chapter two focuses on the women's prison pictures of the 1950s and early 1960s, exploring the psychological depths they added to the genre as a whole. Chapter three looks issues of race, class, gender and sexuality in the prison films most familiar to people, from *The Defiant Ones* to *The Green Mile*. The final section, the Afterword, examines post-9/11 perspectives on incarceration at a time when issues of justice, due process and international law have come under close scrutiny. It further draws attention to issues of mass incarceration, the death penalty, wrongful prosecution and rehabilitation by focusing on both documentaries and fictional narratives.

# 1    PRISON FILMS OF PRE-CODE HOLLYWOOD:
## BIG HOUSES, DEATH HOUSES AND CHAIN GANGS

'Listen, Finn, I'm running this prison, and while I'm running it, I'll run
it without politicians and without bribes. People on the outside are
supposed to be created free and equal, but they aren't. Here they
really are. One inmate's as good as another inmate, but no better.'
                              Warden in *20,000 Years in Sing Sing*

During the Great Depression, and before the enforcement of the Motion
Picture Production Code censorship guidelines, Hollywood churned out
numerous prison films that addressed an alienated America fascinated
with criminality. Headlines both condemned and celebrated gangsters
such as John Dillinger and Al Capone, outlaws who embraced a capitalist
ethos but who played by their own rules to achieve wealth and respect. As
Frank Richard Prassel said of the era, the 'concentration of famous fugi-
tives and their infamous crimes has no equal in the nation's history' (1993:
271). Not surprisingly, Hollywood seized on the criminal's allure and began
producing gangster films that made mobsters their heroes. At virtually the
same time, it began producing prison films, movies that focused not on the
ambitious felon, but on the fallen. Such films appealed because audiences
saw themselves the innocent victims of a corrupt political and economic

system, one that left them feeling trapped in circumstances beyond their control. Such was the hopelessness that even former US President Calvin Coolidge said of the era in 1933, 'In other periods of depression, it has always been possible to see some things which were solid and upon which you could base hope, but as I look about, I now see nothing to give ground for hope' (quoted in Hanson 2008: 139). The screen gangster's violent path to success appealed because it was an anti-heroic fantasy; the prisoner's hopeless plight resonated because it was a felt reality.

Ethan Blue notes that since the nineteenth century, 'convicted criminals had been understood in American law as *civiliter mortuus* — civilly dead. The acts for which they had been convicted and the stigma of criminal conviction placed them largely beyond the pale of public concern' (2012: 2). During the Depression, with its over twenty per cent unemployment rate and myriad workers' strikes resulting in injury and murder with impunity, the status of 'civilly dead' began to be internalised by those who had never actually seen the inside of a prison. Denied the ability to earn a living and incapable of receiving justice, many of the public at large felt fundamentally abandoned and victimised. Hollywood's recognition and exploitation of that sentiment was swift. Thus the prison films of the 1930s depict a seemingly endless parade of men and women cast into big houses, death houses and chain gangs for accidents, minor infractions or crimes they didn't commit. As a character in *Ladies of the Big House* (1931) says of her and her husband's unjust imprisonment, 'What have we ever done to deserve so much pain?'

In tracing the generic origins of the prison film, Bruce Crowther asserts: 'The massive audiences for prison movies in the early 1930s were responding eagerly to a variation on a currently popular theme. These prison movies were simply an off-shoot of the gangster movie genre' (1989: 3). Gangster/prisoner hybrid films like *Each Dawn I Die* (1939) demonstrate the many connections between the two genres. Still, Crowther's claim is highly problematic since George W. Hill's *The Big House* actually *preceded* the three films most often credited with formulating the gangster genre: *The Public Enemy* and *Little Caesar* in 1931 and *Scarface* in 1932. Rather than being an 'off-shoot' of the gangster film, the prison film, if anything, anticipates the gangster film and appears, in many ways, as the gangster film's opposite. The following chart illustrates just some of the ways the two genres are mirror images of each other:

| GANGSTER | PRISONER |
|---|---|
| Pursues the American Dream | American Dream has already failed |
| Appeals because he's bad, corrupt | Appeals because he's good, innocent |
| Has magnetic personality and star power | Is ordinary, often a B-list actor |
| Wants to 'be somebody' | Is a nobody, a number |
| Wants excitement | Wants normalcy |
| A tragic hero, headed for a fall | A fallen soul, seeking redemption |
| A man of action, manic, living for today | A person of inaction, docile, killing time |
| At ease in corruption | Struggles against corruption |
| Bonds with men, females are incidental and a threat to masculinity | Bonds with men, but females essential to salvation and civility |
| Transgressor against the legal system | Sees the legal system as the transgressor |
| Relishes the city and its opportunities | Dreams of retreat to quiet, rural space |
| Shares the same ethos as capitalists | Shares the ethos of labour |
| Takes a spectacular fall so as to discourage emulation (insincere) | Exhibits virtuous behaviour that is meant to be emulated (sincere) |
| Outside the law | At the mercy of the law |
| Shows crime doesn't pay | Shows imprisonment doesn't work |
| Bands with others to break into respectable society | Bands with others to break out of a broken system |
| Often includes symbols of freedom and inclusion, e.g., Statue of Liberty (ironic) | Often begins with symbols of loss of liberty, e.g., walls, chains, fences (sincere) |
| Seeks acceptance through the illegal acquisition of wealth | Seeks acceptance by going legit or giving up the dream of wealth |

Gangsters, such as the Irish Tom Powers in *The Public Enemy* and Italian 'Rico' Bandello in *Little Caesar*, strive for upward mobility in a world that discriminates against them because of their ethnic identities and boorishness. As Jonathan Munby put it:

> The talking gangster openly broached the issues of class and cultural exclusion that had frustrated his ambition... Moreover, in the light of the universal afflictions the Depression brought to American society, the ethnic gangster's struggles with economic and cultural

disenfranchisement resonated with a growing *national* condition. The gangster's tough vernacular voice only enhanced his status as an outspoken representative of the *vox populi*. (1999: 43)

But whereas the gangster films of the 1930s dealt with the societal failures that drove people to commit criminal acts, the prison films of the era focused on the penal system failures that victimised those who were already down on their luck. If the gangster was the representative of the *vox populi*, the prisoner was the representative of the *civiliter mortuus*. Working together, the two genres made the powerful, double-edged argument that society, rather than the individual, needed large-scale reformation.

Rather than drawing primarily from the gangster film, prison films of the early 1930s and beyond combine the narrative modes of the social problem film and melodrama. They tap into melodrama's propensity to 'depict the world as sharply divided into good and evil, with the suffering virtuous people deserving of pathos and admiration' (Kozloff 2014a: 82), and they combine it with the social problem film's desire to 'spotlight a contemporary issue larger than the personal problems of the protagonists' (Kozloff 2014b: 447). Depression-era Hollywood's engagement in the liberal Popular Front movement – what Michael Denning describes as 'the encounter between a powerful democratic social movement … and the modern cultural apparatuses of mass entertainment and education' (1997: xviii) – generated numerous left-leaning 'message' films that were 'ripped from the headlines' and pleaded for social democratisation. As Peter Roffman and Jim Purdy note, in the social problem film, 'the central dramatic conflict revolves around the interaction of the individual with social institutions (such as government, business, political movements, etc)' (1981: viii). During the 1930s, the prison system, with its growing population and shrinking resources, was ripe for criticism.

### Big houses

Prison films almost always criticise current practices of punishment and the political apparatuses that put them in place, as well as the brick and mortar institutions and the authorities who maintain them. The criticisms vary from era to era because the punitive theories are ever-changing and constantly contested. Disciplinary techniques such as corporeal punishment, hard labour and solitary confinement may be popular in one era, while reward, counselling and education may be popular in the next. What seems like innovation and advancement is often a throwback to earlier times. The public shame of the Puritan pillory, for example, might appear centuries later in another form, such as in the case of a Georgia judge who ordered a man to 'spend five weekends in jail and walk around the Fulton County Courthouse for a total of thirty hours wearing a sign that read "I AM A CONVICTED THIEF"' (Book 1999: 654). Derral Cheatwood (1998) argues that prison films can best be understood by viewing them in relation to penal eras. His periodisations include the Depression Era (1929–1942), the Rehabilitation Era (1943–1962), the Confinement Era (1963–1980) and the Administrative Era (1981–1995). Though critics such as Paul Mason (2006) have found Cheatwood's eras too emphatic and artificial, his general approach is useful in showing how pre-Code prison films responded to Depression-era methods of punishment.

The period leading up to the Great Depression is commonly known as the Progressive Era, the compassionate spirit of which was perhaps best embodied by the chairman of the New York State Commission on Prison Reform, Thomas Mott Osborne. Like the plot of a movie, in an effort to fully understand the conditions of prison life at the beginning of the twentieth century, Osborne exchanged his suit and tie for a drab grey uniform, changed his name to Tom Brown, and entered Auburn Prison for six days as prisoner number 33,333x. Although authorities knew his true identity, he insisted on being treated exactly like other inmates. The experience left him shaken, but it also galvanised his efforts to bring about reform to a deplorable system. In his chronicle of the event, *Within Prison Walls*, Osborne described the torturous and maddening state of prison life. He wrote:

> The Prison System does its best to crush all that is strong and good, but you can not always destroy 'that capability and god-like reason' in man. Out of the prison which man has made for his fellow-man, this human cesspool and breeding place of physical, mental and moral disease, emerge a few noble souls, reborn and purified. (1914: 315)

Osborne's experience led to the creation of the New Penology Movement, a series of progressive reforms which he felt could rehabilitate large portions of the prison population. Less than a year later, Osborne was appointed warden of Sing Sing, which at the time of his arrival housed men, often in pairs, in small, dark cells without plumbing and sufficient heating. While at Sing Sing he de-emphasised retribution and implemented new reforms, inspired by the fundamental question he wrote in his book *Society and Prisons: Some Suggestions for a New Penology*: 'Do you wish to produce good prisoners, or prepare good citizens?' (1916: 212). The goals of progressives in penology at this time were to solve societal ills, implement new systems of parole and probation, and individualise the treatment of inmates so that they might have a better chance to succeed in life.

By the time the Great Depression arrived, however, the New Penology Movement was over (largely because of its failure to achieve its goals) and the industrial 'Big House' era had begun. An influential government report, commissioned by Herbert Hoover, entitled *The Report on Penal Institutions, Probation and Parole* concluded that 'the present system is antiquated and inefficient. It does not reform the criminal. It fails to protect society' (quoted in Bosworth 2010: 58). The report brought about several reforms, one of the most significant being the division of prisons into maximum and minimum security institutions. The report also led to the establishment of the Federal Bureau of Prisons to oversee the new system. As Stephen Cox points out, by 1930, the prison population had quadrupled from the time statistics started to be compiled in 1880. He notes:

> The inmate population appeared all the more significant because it tended to be concentrated in prisons that were getting very big. Of the 120,000 American convicts, a large portion were held in a few institutions. A third resided in the federal prisons at Leavenworth, Kansas (3,600), and Atlanta (3,100), and in the state institutions at Columbus, Ohio (4,300); San Quentin, California (4,300); Jackson, Michigan (3,800); Jefferson, Missouri (3,800); Joliet-Stateville, Illinois (3,100); Mansfield, Ohio (2,900); McAlester, Oklahoma (2,500); Folsom, California (2,200); Pendleton, Indiana (2,000), Michigan City, Indiana (2,000); and Chester, Illinois (2,000) (2009: 4–5).

In addition, inmates in 'Big Houses' had little work to do, and rehabilitation programmes all but disappeared. The cells of many of these enormous buildings also became reserved for the nation's most notorious lawbreak-ers, and the public's fascination with criminals began extending to the mysterious buildings in which they were housed. It was in this context that MGM's *The Big House* was produced.

The influence of *The Big House* is difficult to underestimate, initiating as it did a cycle of prison films in pre-Code Hollywood, including *Up the River* (1930), *Numbered Men* (1930), *The Convict's Code* (1930), *Shadow of the Law* (1930), *The Criminal Code* (1931), *Ladies of the Big House*, *20,000 Years in Sing Sing*, *Hell's House* (1932), *The Last Mile* (1932), *I Am a Fugitive from a Chain Gang*, *Hell's Highway* (1932), *Ladies They Talk About* (1932), *Laughter in Hell* (1933) and *The Mayor of Hell* (1933).

*The Big House* begins with the induction of 24-year-old Kent (Robert Montgomery), an ordinary citizen convicted of manslaughter for killing a man while driving drunk on New Year's Eve. After a visit with the warden, he is placed in a cramped cell with a forger, Morgan (Chester Morris), and a brutish murderer, Butch (Wallace Beery). After Butch begins a riot in the cafeteria, he passes a knife under the table to avoid further punishment until it ends up in the hands of Kent. Kent initially hides the knife in his uniform, but when the guards begin inspecting the prisoners and cells, he panics and places it in Morgan's bunk. When the knife is discovered, Morgan, who was set to be released the next day, gets his parole revoked. Morgan soon escapes through the morgue, passing himself off as a dead man. Seeking revenge toward Kent, he tracks down Anne, Kent's sister, who he saw in a photograph while in prison. Anne recognises Morgan from the newspapers and wanted posters but, after pulling a gun on him, decides she doesn't have the heart to turn the seemingly decent escapee in to the authorities. Morgan falls in love with Anne, gets a job and starts living a respectable life, until he is recognised by a detective and returned to prison. Soon after he arrives, Butch tells him of his plan to escape with his gang on Thanksgiving Day. Morgan, however, wants nothing to do with it, insisting that he's going to live a straight life. When Kent learns of Butch's plan, he turns snitch and reports what he knows to the warden in order to gain early release. When Butch's plan is foiled, a full-scale riot breaks out and the convicts take over the prison, capturing many of the guards. Butch threatens to kill the guards one by one unless the prison-ers are released. The warden stands firm, however, and Butch shoots the head guard and tosses his body out for all to see. As tanks begin rolling in, Morgan discovers Kent cowering with the guards in a cell. He decides to spare his life, but Kent, in an act of seeming madness, rushes to the gate, only to be immediately gunned down in the crossfire. Morgan quickly locks the guards in a cell for their own protection, an act that seems to confirm what Butch is told by another inmate, that Morgan was the one who squealed to the warden. Butch seeks out Morgan and shoots him, but Morgan gets off a fatal shot at Butch. After the riot is quelled, Morgan is granted a release for saving the guards. The film ends with Morgan walking out of the prison into the loving arms of Anne.

*The Big House* is such a clear prototype of the prison film that it's easy to mistake its many innovations for clichés, for it has (i) all of the characters (the white-collar criminal introduced to a violent world he doesn't understand, the straightforward felon who has the potential to go straight, the impenitent con, the ineffectual warden, the sadistic guard, the waiting woman, the snitch), (ii) sites (the yard, the hole, the visiting room, the shop, the cafeteria, the warden's office), (iii) sounds (distant train whistles, clanging tin cups, clanking gates, marching feet), and (iv) and situations (the induction process, the warden's speech to the new prisoner, the escape attempt, the riot) found, to varying degree, in virtually every prison movie that follows. Still, as the *New York Times* critic, Mordaunt Hall wrote: 'It is an insight into life in a jail that has never before been essayed on the screen' (1930). That 'insight' was deliberately crafted with a reformist message about overcrowding in mind, so much so that MGM studio head Irving Thalberg hired prison consultant P. W. Garrett to help shape the script with screenwriter Frances Marion and director George Hill. Marion actually toured San Quentin, the prison the film is modelled after, in order to write what she called in her autobiography, 'my rather grim story' (1972: 191). In her article, 'Frances Marion: Censorship and the Screenwriter in Hollywood, 1929–1931', Leslie Kreiner Wilson carefully traces the complicated path Marion had to take 'to create a story that would satisfy prison activists and others alarmed by justice system inequities' (2012: 149). Marion had to please both the Hays Office, who policed for 'immoral' content, and prison reformers, who wanted to actively influence the message of the movie.

Perhaps because of all of the varied interests, *The Big House*'s reformist message is somewhat contradictory if not flat-out murky. Its most blatant critical statement occurs early in the film when Kent meets with the warden, who states: 'I want to warn you against the influences you'll encounter here, or in any other prison. So you be careful of your conduct, your associations. And remember this: prison does not give a man a yellow streak, but if he has one, it brings it out.' After Kent leaves, the old guard, Pop, expresses his concern that Kent is to be housed with hardened criminals Morgan and Butch, stating prophetically: 'He might have a chance in a cell alone.' The sympathetic warden responds: 'Yes, I warned them at the last governor's council. We have three thousand here, and cell accommodations for eighteen hundred. They all want to throw people in prison, but they don't want to provide for them after they are in. You mark my word, Pop, some day we're going to pay for their short-sightedness.'

In the film's overt logic, Kent's demise is caused by his forced association with bad influences Butch and Morgan due to overcrowding. However, that's not what the rest of the story bears out. When Kent first arrives in his cell and Butch steals his cigarettes, he cries out to the guard for help. After the guard walks away, Butch actually gives Kent some good advice (before knocking him out): 'Well, Mister Yellow-belly, you're going to get your first lesson right now. You can't squeal in stir!' Months later, Morgan too gives

Fig. 4: Kent being taught his first lesson by Butch for squealing in *The Big House*.

Kent good advice when he sees him making friends with Oliver, the prison stoolie: 'I'll give you some good advice, Kent. Now, you're in a tough spot, but you've got to learn that whining and double-crossing isn't going to get you anywhere.' Kent replies: 'I'm not whining, and I won't stand for your ribbing. What right have they got to poke me in a cell with Butch and you, a robber, bragging about it.' Even after Morgan recognises Kent's air of superiority, he tells him: 'Too good for the rest of us, huh? Well if you're wise, you'll stand up and take your joe like a regular guy.' Kent, however, refuses to listen and betrays both Morgan and Butch before the film's end, leading to his own demise. He chooses to associate with the rat rather than adopt the convict's code. Kent's problems are his own arrogance and cowardice, not overcrowding. The film may be tacitly critical of giving a young man too harsh a sentence for a single reckless mistake, but Kent is such a thoroughly dislikeable character that he engenders very little sympathy. By the time the movie is over, we see that Kent's death is not so much the tragic result of institutional indifference as the predictable consequence of a deeply flawed character.

This explains, in part, the curious switch in protagonists early in the film. Because of the induction sequence, we are set up to identify with Kent and his struggles to survive, but once he exhibits an irredeemable moral character, we graft onto Morgan, who, though he's made mistakes, shows integrity and the capacity to reform. But the message here is somewhat convoluted as well, as the system is not put on trial so much as the make-up of a man.

In some ways, *The Big House* is a movie not so much about how to treat criminals as it is about how to prevent criminals. And there's a barbed irony to the conclusion it reaches, something hinted at in the opening shot and flatly stated in the conclusion: work. After a credit sequence showing a group of faceless men marching in lockstep, we see an impressive establishing shot of the exterior of the prison. With its massive concrete walls, industrial cellblocks, water tower and billowing smokestacks, the prison clearly resembles a factory, one that produces nothing but idle, unrehabilitated men. Morgan's path to legitimacy is directly connected to his willingness to do meaningful labour, not monotonous hard time. Even while on the lam, he gets a job instead of reverting to his former profession as a forger. When one of the officers pursuing him hears he's gotten a job he says: 'Working? Must be a woman in the case.' His desire to work, however, seems motivated more by self-improvement than by love. When Morgan is eventually caught and returned to prison, the warden tells him: 'You're going to find things tougher than ever here. The state has closed the mill. You know what idleness does to a man.' This may be a direct criticism of the 1929 Hawes Cooper Act, which began limiting the sale of prison-made goods because 'the private sector, labor unions and other groups … argued that the use of prison labor constituted unfair competition' (Verdeyen 1995: 106). The warden even blames the escape attempt on the prisoners' boredom: 'It's three thousand idle men with nothing to do but brood and plot.' Once Morgan is pardoned, he tells the warden he's planning on getting a land grant in the South Pacific so that he can start a plantation, to which the warden responds: 'Good idea. New friends, new surroundings, hard work, that's a man's salvation.' So if work is a man's salvation, idleness, then, must be his ruination. But what is one to do in a country where millions of people are unable to find jobs? It's significant that Morgan has to leave the country to find work, as the American Dream of upward mobility seems all but impossible. Hard work isn't so much the solution as the lack of opportunities are the problem. Old timer Pop's assertion that 'the whole

Fig. 5: *The Big House* prison as idleness factory.

prison system is cockeyed' can be extended to America itself. The prison in *The Big House* is America, an enormous, neglected idleness factory. Morgan is the only one who receives a happy ending because he flees it for a country with more opportunity. Significantly, when he walks through the gates in the final shot, the point-of-view is from inside the prison. Morgan, like everyone else, turns his back on us. As the gates close and the scene fades to black, we are forgotten, simply left behind to do our time.

Though critics have read the film differently, the general consensus is close to that provided by Mike Nellis, who finds within the narrative

> criticism of the official ineptitude which allows reformed men to stay in prison, old cons to corrupt younger ones, and the prison population in general to have so much time on their hands that making each other's lives miserable is the cons' only pastime. This theme, the failure of prison to rehabilitate, together with the scenes of admission to prison and solitary confinement have become integral to the narrative and iconography of subsequent prison films. (Quoted in Wilson and O'Sullivan 2004: 82)

All of these elements left other filmmakers with a paradigm to follow. The cycle of prison films that came after *The Big House* are of varying quality (some are low budget B-pictures), but each added to the vocabulary of the prison film in interesting ways.

The shadow of *The Big House* was even felt by legendary director John Ford, who changed his 1930 production, *Up the River*, from a drama to a 'comedy drama' (as the film's title card tells us) so as not to appear derivative. The Fox Film production marks the feature film debuts of both Humphrey Bogart and Spencer Tracy, the only time they appeared on screen together. The story opens with the escape of Saint Louis (Tracy) and Dannemora Dan (Warren Hymer) from a southern prison. They are later captured and placed in 'A penitentiary in the Middle West', which also houses the upper-middle-class Steve Jordan (Bogart), who becomes Saint Louis' fast friend. Much like Kent in *The Big House*, Jordan is serving a term for accidental manslaughter. The fictional Bensonnata prison, however, houses both male and female inmates, and it is Jordan's job to help induct the women. During one such session, he meets and falls in love with Judy Fields (Claire Luce), who's taking the rap on a stock con for her partner, Frosby (Morgan Wallace). After getting engaged to Judy, Jordan is soon paroled and moves back to New England to live with his mother and sister, who are under the impression that Jordan has been living for years in China. While back home, Frosby arrives and blackmails Jordan into participating in his stock racket until Jordan becomes enraged when Frosby starts defrauding his mother. Word soon gets back to Saint Louis, who escapes with Dan during a prison variety show. The two men make it to Jordan just in time to prevent him from killing Frosby and ruining his future with Judy, who is set to be paroled in a few months. After stealing Jordan's mother's bonds back from Frosby, the two escapees hop a train and make it back to the prison just in time to participate in the big baseball game against a rival prison. The film ends 'happily' as Saint Louis and Dan convince the warden to let them take the field.

Although the plot may sound ridiculous (and it is), the film is significant for several reasons. First, it showed the versatility of the genre by incorporating elements of comedy and the backstage musical. The variety show sequence, which includes an unsettling blackface performance intercut with close-ups of a black prisoner laughing hysterically, lasts over ten minutes.

Scenes of inmates performing for one another have appeared in many films, most notably in Jean Renoir's masterful *Grand Illusion* (1937). Such performances serve numerous functions. At their most basic, songs and skits are ways for the prisoners to escape the harsh realities of prison. But the stage is also a site where prisoners can perform alternative identities (such as blackface) and challenge notions of masculinity that might otherwise be viewed as threatening (the prisoners in *Grand Illusion* and *Up the River*, for example, both appear in drag). Performances also suspend or alter power relationships. The tough guy in the yard may become the fool on stage, just as the servile inmate may suddenly become the director in charge. Performances by inmates, as well as other forms of entertainment, are frequently used to distract the guards from their regular duties so that violence or an escape might take place. As Nicole Rafter notes, 'Convicts in *Each Dawn I Die* use the weekly movie as an occasion to knock off their enemies, as they do again half a century later in *In the Name of the Father* (1993)' (2006: 167). Although the incorporation of the baseball game in *Up the River* seems merely a narrative contrivance, it too reinforces the all-pervasive theme of escapism in prison films. The peripheral game in

*Up the River* would later become the *central* conceit of Robert Aldrich's *The Longest Yard*, which uses a climactic football game between the cons and guards to realign familiar roles, transform everyday drudgery, and instill in the prisoners a sense of dignity and respect, however temporary.

Even though *Up the River* builds on the familiar iconography and *mise-en-scène* of the prison film by its inclusion of cramped cells, the yard and a noir-like escape sequence, its overall feel is one of unreality. The majority of scenes are shot on studio sets not nearly as elaborate as those in *The Big House*, and the many absurd details and contrivances detract from any sense of authenticity: the warden's nine-year-old daughter plays unsupervised with the male inmates, a prisoner performs a knife-throwing act during the variety show, a zebra-striped mule wanders the yard, etc. Similarly, its incorporation of women inmates housed in communal living areas provides an early glimpse of spaces and situations depicted more thoroughly in films like *Caged* (1950) and *I Want to Live!* (1958), but the easy interactions between male and female inmates is purely fictional. Stephen Cox notes: 'Women were sent to prison during the Big House period, but … they were sent in much smaller numbers than men' (2009: 14). They were also isolated from the men and 'dispatched to all-female institutions often intended to resemble "homes", "cottages", or other "family" environments. They lived in the Small House, not the Big House' (ibid.). Like many women in later films, Judy finds herself in prison for getting involved with the wrong man, and she finds her redemption by landing the right one. The film's inclusion of the welfare worker, Mrs. Massey (Louise Mackintosh), establishes the presence of agencies advocating for the well-being of prisoners, but she is portrayed as an ineffectual fool who merely hands out fashion magazines to the women and unwittingly passes notes between Steve and Judy. As in *The Big House*, the prisoners rehabilitate themselves by embracing the lofty values of loyalty, self-sacrifice and love. Although *Up the River* shows examples of injustice and corruption, any reformist message is limited to personal redemption. The film is not particularly interested in systemic change. In fact, it displays an overt validation of existing conditions through its promotion of patriotism. Images of baseball, hayrides and small-town life pervade the picture, and the repeated playing of 'Hooray for the Red, White and Blue' by the prison band undermines any real critical impulse that might have been existent in the original, dramatic script. In this way, *Up the River* is *The Big House*'s opposite. Whereas one is interested in portraying the American nightmare, the other is interested in promoting the American ideal.

Howard Hawks' *The Criminal Code* (1931) renewed the semi-reformist zeal of *The Big House* and is in many ways more memorable than its predecessor, in part because of Boris Karloff's menacing performance and Hawks' innovative uses of sound, extended shots and montage. Filmed on some of the same sets as *The Big House* and based on a play by Martin Flavin (who also wrote some of the dialogue for *The Big House*), the film, according to Hawks' biographer Todd McCarthy, was deliberately 'keyed to exposing prison conditions and advocating penal reform' (1997: 118). In the film, Robert Graham (Phillips Holmes) is a naïve, good kid who accidentally kills a man in a speakeasy in an attempt to protect the honour of a prostitute (played by Mary Doran). By-the-book district attorney, Mark Brady (Walter Huston), is sympathetic but won't drop the charges because 'somebody's got to pay', in part because 'the yellow press' loves 'the smell of blood'. Like Kent and Jordan before him, Graham gets ten years in the penitentiary as punishment for manslaughter. The politically ambitious Brady's insistence on prosecution and his boast that he could have gotten Graham off if he were his defence attorney make clear an arbitrary system of justice.

Rather than taking the viewer through the induction process, the film jumps forward six years by means of a stylish montage of marching prisoners and shows the toll incarceration has taken on Graham. After working for years in the prison's noisy jute mill, Graham is a broken man, brought to near madness by politics, media and the criminal justice system. Before completely losing his mind, however, Graham is assigned to be the driver of the new warden, Brady, who also brings along his daughter, Mary (Constance Cummings). In the meantime, the film's true villain, Runch (Clark Marshall), rats out his fellow prisoners and gets one of them killed during an escape attempt. When Graham's cellmate, Ned Galloway (Boris Karloff), learns of Runch's betrayal, he kills him in a masterfully shot, tension-filled sequence. Because of Graham's proximity to the murder scene, Brady is certain Graham knows the culprit. When Graham refuses to give the name, Brady, who'd been working to get Graham a pardon, places him in 'the dungeon' with only bread and water until he does so. Rather than being a merely punitive act, however, the rough treatment is actually an attempt by Brady to protect Graham from being prosecuted for the murder.

Fig. 6: Ned Galloway (Boris Karloff) in cold-blooded pursuit of the prison snitch, Runch, in *The Criminal Code*.

Brady decides to put pressure on him until such time as he decides to sacrifice a fellow inmate and save himself. In an attempt to get her father to stop, Mary, who confesses to having fallen in love with Graham, states, 'What good is it to save a man if you destroy him while you're doing it?' It's at this point that both Brady and Graham are forced to contemplate their respective 'criminal codes'. Both are flawed, paradoxical and inherently unfair. Graham is eventually exonerated and reunited with Mary, but the law and what's right are revealed throughout the film to be deeply incompatible. There is more honour in upholding the criminal code than the legal code, a sharp irony that effectively condemns the entire criminal justice system.

## The death house

An even darker meditation on punishment appeared in Samuel Bischoff's low-budget B-movie, *The Last Mile*, a film about death row inmates that the

*New York Times* critic called 'grim and gruesome' (Hall 1932). According to the Death Penalty Information Center,

> From the 1920s to the 1940s, there was a resurgence in the use of the death penalty. This was due, in part, to the writings of criminologists, who argued that the death penalty was a necessary social measure. In the United States, Americans were suffering through Prohibition and the Great Depression. There were more executions in the 1930s than in any other decade in American history, an average of 167 per year. (2016)

*The Last Mile*'s blunt foreword by Lewis Lawes, the warden of Sing Sing, addressed the problem and set the film's bleak tone:

> 'The Last Mile' is more than a story of prison and of the condemned. To me it is a story of those men within barred cells, crushed mentally, physically and spiritually between unrelenting forces of man-made laws and man-fixed death. And justly or unjustly found guilty, are they not the victims of man's imperfect conventions, upon which he has erected a social structure of doubtful security? What is society's responsibility for ever-increasing murders? What shall be done with the murderers? 'The Last Mile' does not pretend to give an answer. Society must find its own solution. But murder on the heels of murder is *not* that solution.

Based on a Broadway play by John Wexley, the film tells the story of Richard Walters (Howard Phillips), who has been unjustly sentenced to death for the murder of his gas station business partner, Max. In front of a police officer, Walters had confronted Max over his withdrawing of funds from the business. When they are robbed moments later, one of the thieves pulls the trigger of a gun in Walters' hand, subsequently killing Max. Hearing the shot, the officer reappears just in time to see Walters hunched over Max's body with the gun still in his hand. The rest of the film takes place in the death house, where the numbered inmates wait in agony for their turns to be executed in the electric chair. Eventually number four, John 'Killer' Mears (Preston Foster), gets hold of a guard's gun and begins an escape attempt. Mears and the other men take over the death house and Mears begins killing the guards one by one until he has the assurance from the warden that he'll be provided an escape vehicle. During a full-scale battle between the guards and the prisoners, Walters learns that the governor has issued him a stay of execution because new evidence has been found that will likely exonerate him. When Mears is finally killed and the escape attempt thwarted, authorities determine that Walters wasn't responsible for the riot. The governor issues him a full pardon, and he is released to his mother.

Although the second half of the film turns into a somewhat run-of-the-mill action picture, the first half's sombre, existential focus on the torturous psychological effects of waiting to die set the film apart from its predecessors. When Walters first arrives at the death house, he's not treated by the other inmates as 'fresh fish'; rather, there is an instant camaraderie among the men. They all await the same fate together. Even the warden is kindly, stating: 'We'll do everything in our power to make you comfortable. You can have anything that you want, within the rules.' A half an hour after Walters arrives, number one, Joe Berg (George E. Stone) is slated to die, and the countdown creates mental torment for the entire house. As the only African-American inmate, number two (played by Daniel L. Hayes), begins to sing a plaintive spiritual, Berg paces nervously in his cell. When the lights flicker from the testing of the chair, Berg begins to break down, but Mears shouts his support: 'Don't lose yourself, one!' The entire procedure is an exercise in sadism, exemplified most clearly by the tauntings of the ruthless death house guard, Drake (Albert J. Smith). The ritualistic preparation of the chair, last meal and visit from the rabbi are all things the condemned men have been forced to witness before. There is little of the masculine posturing and reluctance to show weakness evident in prior prison films. When Walters confesses he's going to be sick, he says: 'I guess I'm yella'; to which Mears replies, 'Yella, nothin'. My belly's been turnin' over for an hour.' As Berg's time finally arrives, he states: 'I hate to go, but I guess it's gotta be done.' The methodical nature of the proceedings, however, reveals that the execution doesn't, in fact, *have to* be done; each individual involved consciously chooses to perform his task and has the power to refuse. Later in the film, the priest, Father O'Connor (Alec B. Francis), tells Mears that the warden had to let the guards die just as he has to carry out the execution orders, saying: 'That's his job, his duty.' The film shows that this blind devotion to duty has led to a barbaric system,

Fig. 7: Mad prisoner number eight wailing in *The Last Mile*.

one made up of functionaries — lawyers, judges, guards, priests — who collude to perform their roles without question. In such a system, basic humanity is supplanted by the artificial need to follow orders.

*The Last Mile* stands apart because it does more than explore previous prison movie themes; it makes a clear (though some may say heavy-handed) argument against the penal system and the death penalty in particular. It also brings to the foreground elements of the prison movie that were previously peripheral. Madness, for example, appears in *The Big House* in the form of a wild-eyed inmate who thinks cockroaches are butterflies and prison slop is tenderloin steak, but his character is used primarily for comedic effect. *The Criminal Code*'s Galloway appears mad when carrying out the murder of the stoolie Runch, but his temporary mania is aroused more from personal betrayal than institutional mistreatment. *The Last Mile*, however, shows the madness of the system by featuring prisoner number eight, Eddie Werner (Paul Fix), who has been driven insane from his time in the death house. Frequently throughout the film, his plaintive wails punctuate the silence and fuel the anxiety of the other inmates. Even though he has been given a stay of execution because of insanity, the officials deliberately leave him on death row to torture the other inmates. As Mears explains: 'They don't take him out, they leave him here so he can drive us all nuts.'

Clocks also feature in the foreground in *The Last Mile*. In both *The Big House* and *Up the River*, a large clock is shown in the background of the yard above the gates. It not only keeps the prisoners on a strict schedule, but it also reminds them that they are wasting their lives and killing time. The torment of the clock is used to much greater effect in *The Last Mile*. The mere presence of the clock on death row creates dread as the prisoners count down their last remaining days and hours. Images of clocks and watches pervade the film, connecting one scene to another and appearing in multiple locations, such as the warden's office and the governor's desk. Not coincidentally, it is Walters' pocket watch, found by the police on the body of one of the robbers, which confirms his story and sets him free. The symbol of tyranny becomes a symbol of freedom, and when his watch is discovered, time is, quite literally, returned to him.

Finally, *The Last Mile* foregrounds most clearly a characteristic found in many prison films: the patriarchal veneration of mothers. Drawing on the traditions of what E. Ann Kaplan calls 'the maternal sacrifice melodrama', the film provides a prime example of 'the "angel" mother-figure' (1992: 13) in the character of Walters' mother (Louise Carter). Andrea S. Walsh identifies the trope as originating in women's fiction, radio soap operas and silent melodramas, narratives 'featuring noble, sacrificial … mothers valiantly encountering crisis upon crisis' (1984: 90). Even though Walters owns his own business, he still lives with his mother, who cooks and cleans for him, and it is she who sticks faithfully by his side during the trial, cries out in agony when he is convicted, and fights tirelessly for his exoneration. Smaller but significant references to mothers appear in earlier prison films as well. In *The Big House*, Butch receives a letter informing him that his mother has died. It is a scene of genuine pathos as he tearfully recounts to Morgan how she was the only person who ever really cared for him. His decision to break out of prison, which comes immediately after he hears the news of her death, is motivated in part by guilt and a desire to pay her back for all she sacrificed. He tells Morgan: 'I'm gonna give that little old lady the swellest funeral she ever had.' A similar scene appears in *The Criminal Code*. While playing a game of checkers with his cellmate, Graham reads a telegraph telling him his mother has passed away. After hanging his head in a long silence, he says tearfully: 'She used to come to see me, every Friday. My mother was awful nice.' His cellmate's only reaction is to nod at the board and say: 'Your move, kid', a clear indication that motherly devotion and maternal tenderness are over. In *Up the River*, Jordan hides his incarceration from his mother and returns to her after his release. During the variety show, one of the young inmates sings 'M-O-T-H-E-R' ('M is for the million things she gave me...') to a weeping audience, filmed in close-ups to underscore the men's anguish and adoration. In an odd moment in Rowland Brown's *Hell's Highway*, inmate Duke Ellis (Richard Dix) even gives his mother a welcoming, lingering kiss on the mouth during visitation. *The Last Mile* establishes the importance of mothers at the outset by playing 'Ave Maria', the Catholic prayer calling for the divine intervention of the blessed mother, during the sombre foreword. While in the death house, Walters expresses unshakable faith in his mother's ability to get him a stay of execution, stating: 'Mothers never fail'.

Interestingly, mothers in these pre-Code prison pictures are not revealed to be the sources of their sons' failures, as they are in later films like *White Heat* (1949), where, as Lucy Fischer states, 'insanity's cause' in Cody Jarrett (James Cagney) is 'embodied in the figure of Mother' (1996: 94). Rather, mothers are the embodiments of unconditional love and devotion. Their lives testify to a goodness that still exists in the world, and their solitary deaths and sufferings signify the perversion of the family order caused by the prison system. These mothers live for their sons. As such, they are not complex characters with lives of their own, and idealising them perpetuates the long-standing, self-serving patriarchal construct of woman as self-sacrificing nurturer. In some prison films, such as *The Criminal Code*, those roles may be transferred to wives and girlfriends in an optimistic ending. In others, however, the mother-role remains unfulfilled, creating a kind of ideal absence that takes on a metaphysical status. When the prisoner in *Up the River* sings that 'mother' is 'a word that means the world to me', the deep sadness on the faces of the men imparts an understanding that that world is gone forever.

## Chain gangs

Of all the methods of punishment implemented in America, none has a more shameful history than that of the chain gang. Emerging in the South after the Civil War and lasting well into the 1950s, the chain gang was little other than a legalised extension of slavery, an immoral subjugation of blacks that produced forced labour, retribution and human misery. As Abby Stein summarises the system:

> Freed Blacks in the Southern states were arrested on spurious legal charges, convicted, chained, tortured, and forced into a life of involuntary servitude for a variety of industries that were remaking the Southern economy from a slave-based one into free market model. Conviction rates eerily reflected the ebb and flow of small local businesses' need for laborers and it was all perfectly legal. (2012: 256)

To be sure, whites were forced into labour as well, but chain gangs were overwhelmingly composed of southern blacks. Although prison overcrowding and torment are subjects addressed in many prison films, notably absent from the films of the 1930s is any direct acknowledgement of the decade's rising rate of African-American incarceration. As Scott Christianson notes:

> From 1925 to 1939 the nation's rate of imprisonment climbed from 79 to 137 per 100,000 residents. In large measure, this growth was driven by greater incarceration of [African-Americans]. Indeed, one scholar noticed that during the period between 1930 and 1936 black incarceration rates had risen substantially to a level about three times greater than those for whites. (1998: 229)

In an attempt to capitalise on the success of films like *The Big House* and address the problem of chain gangs, Warner Bros. purchased the rights to Robert Elliott Burns' autobiographical account of his time in a Georgia chain gang and produced the decade's quintessential social problem film: *I Am a Fugitive from a Chain Gang*. In his autobiography, Jack Warner referred to the movie as 'the first sermon I had ever put on film' (1964: 218). But even though Warner's cinematic sermon exposed the immorality of chain gangs by exploiting the social problem film's propensity to 'place enormous stress on the protagonist's suffering' (Kozloff 2014b: 460), that suffering, as in the decade's first chain gang movie *Hell's Highway*, was limited almost exclusively to white suffering.

Both *I Am a Fugitive from a Chain Gang* and *Hell's Highway* provide more sympathetic images of incarcerated blacks than any prison film prior, but they centre their stories on the struggles of white protagonists. In *I Am a Fugitive from a Chain Gang*, James Allen (Paul Muni) is a World War I veteran who returns home to his mother and reverend brother (played by Louise Carter and Hale Hamilton, respectively). Immediately pressed by his family and former boss to take a dull clerical position in the local shoe factory, Allen reveals that his time in the service has changed him. No longer content to work in a meaningless job, Allen sets out to 'find himself' and pursue his dream of becoming an engineer. After wandering the country looking for work, he is nearly penniless. When another man in a southern flophouse offers to buy Allen a hamburger at a nearby diner, he jumps at the chance, only to be embroiled in the man's scheme to rob the restaurant. Forced at gunpoint to empty the till, Allen panics and attempts to escape when the police arrive. He is soon captured, convicted and given ten years' hard labour on the chain gang. In addition to being whipped and fed slop, he is forced to work from sun up to sun down, busting rocks and dismantling a railroad. Finding the conditions brutal and intolerable, he hatches a daring escape plan and successfully enacts it. After landing in Chicago, Allen (now 'Allen James') spends years moving up the ladder of a construction company, eventually ending up a wealthy engineer and one of the most respected men in the city. Soon after his arrival, Allen begins seeing the proprietor of his boarding house, Marie Woods (Glenda Farrell), who ultimately blackmails him into marriage when she discovers his true identity. While suffering a sham marriage, Allen meets a woman named Helen (Helen Vinson) and soon falls in love with her. Feeling trapped yet again and unable to go along with the charade, Allen dares Marie to turn him in, which she subsequently does. After a lengthy, public extradition battle pitting northern justice against southern, Allen accepts a plea deal, agreeing to serve ninety days in prison while working a desk job, after which he will be paroled. He soon discovers he's been double-crossed and is forced to serve out the remainder of his original sentence on the chain gang. He escapes again, however, and is not heard from for months, until he visits Helen back on the streets of Chicago. Now paranoid and anxious, Allen confesses he just needed to see her one more time. When she offers him money to survive, he refuses, then disappears into the darkness.

*I Am a Fugitive from a Chain Gang* is remembered primarily for inciting public outrage against chain gangs and contributing to their demise. As David A. Davis points out, however, the system remained unaltered for many years after the film's release and the leasing of convicts only ended when the southern economy changed. He writes:

> Tellingly, the system changed in response to economic forces that rendered the direct exploitation of human bodies unprofitable. In other words, the chain gang, not unlike the chain gang movie, functioned within a matrix of economic factors involving supply, demand, labor, and capital. Humanity and depravity factored into the equation only to the extent that they impacted material conditions. (2010: 408)

Still, the film made an indelible impact on the public imagination, and 'the South's peculiar penal system became a signifier of its moral depravity, along with sharecropping, segregation, and lynching' (2010: 399). The images of shackles, leg irons and whips made clear the point that slavery was not over. Though black and white prisoners work side by side, the black actors who appear in the film are relegated mostly to the background. In one scene, viewers are shown tight close-ups of despondent white and black prisoners alike waiting to be driven to work, suggesting a kind of democracy of despair. The camp, however, is segregated, and because the film focuses on Allen, viewers never see the black barracks where one can only imagine the greater horrors that occur there. The one small speaking roll given to a black actor also reverts to the stereotype of the menacing, muscle-bound 'black buck'. While working on the rocks, one inmate points to a muscular, shirtless black inmate named Sebastian (Everett Brown) and tells Allen admiringly, 'Look at that big buck swing that sledge!' Significant too is the fact that Allen convinces Sebastian to use his sledge hammer to help loosen his leg irons, thus relegating him to the stereotypical role of the self-sacrificing black attendant who exists solely to aid the white protagonist, for surely Sebastian could have loosened his own leg irons.

Similarly, the portrayals of black prisoners in *Hell's Highway* consist mostly of caricatures. The many work songs and ballads sung by the segregated black prisoners are the most realistic facets of the film, as they

Fig. 8: Black prisoners waiting to be transported for hard labour in *I Am a Fugitive from a Chain Gang*.

induce authentic feelings of plaintiveness in the viewer. As with *I Am a Fugitive from a Chain Gang*, however, this true poignancy is relegated to the background, essentially becoming the soundtrack to white misfortune.

In many ways, *Hell's Highway* seems derivative of the much more refined *I Am a Fugitive from a Chain Gang*, even though it was released a few months before it. Both films' protagonists are World War I veterans, 'forgotten men' who have been abandoned by the country for whom they served. When Duke (Richard Dix) exposes his back for a whipping in *Hell's Highway*, even the sadistic warden pauses upon seeing a large American flag tattoo with '167th INF.' written below it. Allen is similarly whipped in *I Am a Fugitive from a Chain Gang*, but the more poignant scene occurs when he tries to pawn his military award for bravery, only to be shown a large glass case filled with similarly discarded medals. The critique of neglected veterans is obvious, but it also alludes to a larger theme found in these early prison movies, that of silence and miscommunication. Just as Duke and Allen have fallen through the cracks and remain unheard by the very authorities who should have their welfare in mind, so too are many prisoners unable to articulate themselves at even the smallest levels. In *The Big House*, Butch is illiterate, another man is insane, and yet another has a severe stutter. *Up the River* includes an illiterate inmate and a prisoner who mumbles incoherently. In *The Criminal Code*, when all attempts to express dissent through language fail, the prisoners resort to a deafening, nonverbal yammering as a method of protest. In death row movies like *The Last Mile*, miscommunications such as calls that don't reach the warden's office in time can lead to death. These forgotten prisoners are often as unable to speak as they are to be heard.

In her cogent essay on *I Am a Fugitive from a Chain Gang*, Kristen Whissel points out 'the Classical Hollywood prison film's indebtedness to melodrama' (2015: 82). For Whissel, 'The prison film's melodramatic imagination helped form and re-form popular understandings of excessive and "just" modes of modern punishment' (ibid.). According to Thomas Elsaesser, melodramas, which are typically female-centred, often portray women trapped in oppressive, domestic spaces, 'helplessly struggling inside their emotional prisons' (2012: 459). Such material and emotional sensibilities are readily adaptable to prison narratives, which show inmates trapped in oppressive, institutional spaces, helplessly struggling to survive. As Elsaesser further notes, the responsibility for the situations characters find themselves in

> is firmly placed on a social and existential level, away from the arbitrary and finally obtuse logic of private motives and individualized psychology. This is why melodrama, at its most accomplished, seems capable of reproducing more directly than other genres the patterns of domination and exploitation existing in a given society. (2012: 457)

In the majority of pre-Code prison films, individuals are the victims of external forces beyond their control, a theme that runs counter to the dominant ideology of American individualism. Though the pre-Code films primarily portrayed prisoners as victims, they established the debates about societal blame and personal responsibility, as well as the need for reform or retribution. These debates would be further explored in the decade's later films, such as *Road Gang* (1936), *San Quentin* (1937), *Prison Nurse* (1938) and *Each Dawn I Die*.

While drawing on the genre conventions of the social problem film and melodrama, the litany of wrongly-convicted men in these early prison films also anticipates the existential bleakness of film noir, expressed most succinctly by Tom Neal's character, Al, in the 1945 film, *Detour*. While contemplating his culpability in the accidental killing of a man named Haskell, he states: 'I keep trying to forget what happened. And wonder what my life might have been if that car of Haskell's hadn't stopped. But one thing I don't have to wonder about. I know. Someday a car will stop to pick me up that I never thumbed. Yes, fate, or some mysterious force, can put the finger on you or me for no good reason at all.' The difference between noir and prison films, however, is that even though prison films show a world where anyone can be convicted for no good reason at all, they also often suggest pathways to redemption. Sometimes those pathways are personal, sometimes they're institutional, and sometimes they're both.

Guard one: 'I want to catch that last show at The Bijou.'
Guard two: 'That prison movie?'
Guard one: 'Yeah.'
Guard two: 'They never get things right in prison pictures.'
Guard one: 'I know, but I like to pick out the flaws.'

*Women's Prison* (1955)

Movies featuring women in prison date back almost as far as their male counterparts. Cecil B. DeMille's silent film, *The Godless Girl* (1929), for example, tells the story of a young atheist girl and a devout Christian boy who instigate a riot during an atheist meeting. When a student is killed in the chaos, Judy (Lina Basquette) and Bob (Tom Keene) are held responsible and sentenced to the same brutal prison reformatory. Though primarily a love story and conversion narrative (Judy comes to believe at least in the possibility that 'Someone is running things!'), the film shares many features with a typical prison movie: an induction sequence, a riot, an escape attempt, a sadistic guard and abuse. Like many of the films that follow it, *The Godless Girl* carries a reformist message, including a rather blunt statement in the middle of the film: 'The incidents of this story are true. These conditions actually exist in certain reformatories. There are many others, however, that are humane and progressive – thanks to those who are striving to help our Delinquent Youth to become good men and women.' Other significant pre-Code films showing women in prison include *Ladies of the Big House*, *Ladies They Talk About* and *The Sin of Nora Moran* (1933). Although the last film is a low-budget production from Majestic Pictures, telling the story of a woman sitting on death row for murdering the man who sexually abused her, it is particularly fascinating for its complicated narrative structure, including flashbacks, flashbacks within flashbacks, hypnotic visions and opiate-induced hallucinations. Although these early films established some of the norms of the women's prison film, it wasn't until the Cold War era of the 1950s and early 1960s that the subgenre truly began to distinguish itself from its male counterpart.

In the aftermath of World War II, attention to external military battles quickly yielded to internal ideological battles as America reacted to profound social, political and economic changes that seemed to threaten the nation. One of the most significant of those changes involved gender roles. Women who had found economic independence and value in the workforce during the war were strongly encouraged to give up those freedoms and return to the home. Men who experienced both the traumas and excitements of war were suddenly urged to work unsatisfying desk jobs in a growing number of corporations. Although men were the titular heads of the nuclear household, women were the 'engineers' of the domestic space. The situation left many women feeling disenfranchised and isolated, and many men feeling subservient at work and emasculated at home. The publications of the Kinsey reports on male and female sexuality, in 1948 and 1953 respectively, further exacerbated anxieties over sex and gender, as Kinsey's research revealed that there were no clear norms of sexual behaviour, destabilising even the most intimate aspects of selfhood. These findings, combined with nuclear fears, Cold War paranoia and uncertainties about where the world was headed (as well as what it had just come out of), created deep anxieties about identity, family and overall security. In response, movies, television and magazines worked relentlessly to contain such fears through the promotion of 'normalcy' and the condemnation of 'deviance'. As Alan Nadel writes in *Containment Culture*, the period from 1946 to 1964 was a time when

'conformity' became a positive value in and of itself. The virtue of conformity – to some idea of religion, to 'middle-class' values, to distinct gender roles and rigid courtship rituals – became a form of public knowledge through the pervasive performances of and allusions to containment narratives. (1995: 4)

Women's prison pictures, with their portrayals of 'fallen' women, failed mothers and sexual 'degenerates', emerged as the ultimate narratives of containment, cautionary tales depicting the consequences of not adhering to the 'virtue of conformity'. Interestingly, though, key films like *Caged* (1950), *Women's Prison* (1955), *I Want to Live!* and *House of Women* (1962) paradoxically challenged the very condemnations they revealed, making them both complicit in and subversive of the cultural milieu of conformity.

*Ladies and tramps*

One of the most revealing and frightening portrayals of prison in the 1950s comes from a very unlikely source: Walt Disney's *Lady and the Tramp* (1955). After staying out all night with Butch, the mutt from the wrong side of the tracks, the purebred, upper-class Lady finds herself in the dog pound, ostensibly jailed for the crime of, basically, premarital sex. Surrounded by lower-class social outcasts (such as the homeless Nutsy, the Communist Borzoi and the 'loose' Peg), Lady begins to understand just how far she has fallen for channeling her newly-discovered sexual maturity (her 'license') in the wrong direction. The proper role of females, according to the film, is to promise sexual gratification to the male only after he agrees to 'settle down' and raise a family. As Nadel writes, 'the responsibility attached to her sexual license and the cult of domesticity that that responsibility entails, defines the difference between Lady and Tramp' (1995: 120). According to Nadel, then, the title of the film should more properly be 'Lady or a Tramp', an appellation that reveals 'the two sexual roles available to 1950s females' (1995: 118). Lady's shame is further revealed when she returns home, seemingly pregnant from her reckless evening. In an effort to return her to some level of respectability, both of the older, upper-class neighbour dogs, Trusty and Jock, offer her their paws in marriage. Even as she rejects their proposals, her salvation is dependent upon persuading Butch to give up his carefree lifestyle for one of responsibility. In typical Disney fashion, she succeeds, leading to a happy ending where Lady and Butch, surrounded by a litter of puppies, join Lady's owners, Jim Dear and Darling, in domestic bliss.

The majority of incarcerated women in the films of the 1950s, however, do not share Lady's eventual good fortune. Lady's success is tied, in part, to her ability to learn from her mistakes. Even more important, however, is the presence of a man (or dog, in this case) willing to step up and do the right thing. Such men are remarkably absent from the majority of women's prison movies, which focus instead on the relationships between women and the harm men cause women. Many kindly doctors materialise to aid women with pregnancies and in coping with prison life in general, but on the whole, the lack of husbands and boyfriends to support and 'legitimise' fallen women is pronounced, and in no film is the absence of support more profoundly felt than in John Cromwell's *Caged*.

Written by Virginia Kellogg, *Caged* is based on her story 'Women Without Men', which she produced after spending time in several women's prisons. The film opens with nineteen-year-old Marie (Eleanor Parker) arriving at the Women's State Prison and hearing a guard say: 'Pile out, you tramps, it's the end of the line.' During the induction sequence, Marie discloses that she has been convicted of being an accessory to a gas station robbery. Sentenced to one-to-fifteen years, she explains she merely rushed to her husband's aid when she saw the attendant hit him over the head. As the matron types up her statement, she tells Marie: 'five bucks less and it wouldn't be a felony', underscoring the arbitrary nature of her punishment. During the induction physical, Marie learns she is two months pregnant. Her first chance for parole, however, comes up in ten months. Because her husband was killed during the robbery, she must convince her mother to take the baby for three months or else it will be put up for adoption. Though she has difficulty adjusting to prison life and the sadistic guard, Harper (Hope Emerson), she is determined to serve her time quietly, refusing offers by fellow inmate, Kitty Stark (Betty Garde), to get her a job 'boosting' (shoplifting) for the racket once she gets out of prison. Despite assurances by the humane warden, Ruth Benton (Agnes Moorehead), that she has a good shot at parole, Marie begins to lose hope when she sees fellow inmate June (Olive Deering) commit suicide after being denied parole. Upon the shock of the discovery, Marie goes into labour and gives birth to a healthy child; but because her step-father refuses to let her mother take the baby for even a few months, Marie eventually loses the child to the state. After being denied parole, the tone of her voice begins to lose its sweetness and she grows increasingly bitter. Soon after, 'vice queen'

Elvira Powell (Lee Patrick) arrives and, in order to take control of the ward, convinces Harper to place Kitty in solitary. Later, Marie discovers a kitten in the yard and hides it in her bunk. When Harper tries to take it away from her, the women begin to riot, and the kitten is killed in the turmoil. In a brutal scene, Harper then drags Marie into her quarters and shaves her head in retaliation. Benton wants Harper fired, but because Harper has connections in high places, she retains her position, and Warden Benton is asked to resign instead. Upon demanding a public hearing on the abuses and corruption in the prison, the commissioner backs down and Benton is allowed to keep her job. After a month in solitary, Kitty emerges mentally disturbed and kills Harper in the cafeteria by stabbing her repeatedly with a fork. During the murder, Marie begins urging her on, shouting: 'Kill her, kill her, kill her!' Completely jaded by all that she's been through and desperately wanting parole, Marie agrees to take a 'cashier's job' for Elvira. Upon her release, she has one last conversation with Warden Benton who asks her why, when she was so close to living a clean life, she decided to work for Elvira's gang. After serving 502 days, Marie throws her wedding ring in the trash and tells the warden: 'You can't lick the system.' She then exits the prison and joins two men in the back of an expensive car. When one of the men places his hand on her knee, it's clear that Marie has become both a prostitute and habitual criminal.

Like many of the men's prison films of the 1930s, *Caged* draws upon melodrama and the social problem film, but in a more stylised and self-conscious fashion, which often tips toward camp. Camp, as Susan Sontag famously defined it, employs 'artifice and exaggeration' to foster 'a double sense in which some things can be taken' (2008: 45). *Caged*'s theatrical trailer, for example, adopts an earnest approach to its subject matter akin to investigative journalism while simultaneously articulating that pursuit in florid, overwrought language: 'Warner Bros. reveals the menace that turns today's first offenders into tomorrow's legion of the lost.' The voice-over further states: 'Each day the criminal court condemns scores of unfortunate girls to prisons that need reforming more than the prisoners. For in these dismal cages, the first-time loser is exposed to the habitual criminal by a vicious, outmoded penal system.' Such clashes, which occur throughout the film itself, throw viewers off balance and make them question the film's real intent. Is the movie a sincere condemnation of 'bad girls' and the current penal system, or is it a subversive examination of a society that ascribes strict gender identities to women, limits their economic opportunities, and then punishes them for their 'moral failures'? The answer, of course, is both.

*Caged* establishes this duality from the start, opening from the point of view of the back of a prison transport truck. In noir-like fashion, the shot is almost entirely black, except for a small caged frame through which we see the outside world rushing away. Though the striking visuals dominate the shot, the more significant detail is the screaming siren that overwhelms the powerful Max Steiner score. Sirens, used to rush to the scene of a crime, serve no legitimate purpose in this context since the crimes are over. Director John Cromwell employs a backwards logic from the outset, one that foreshadows the film's larger exploration of systemic inversion. 'The system' that Marie says she 'can't lick' causes good women to turn bad, devout mothers to abandon their children, and straight women to invert their sexuality (late nineteenth- and early twentieth-century sexologists frequently used the term 'sexual inversion' to mean homosexuality). As Kitty tells Marie while lying next to her in bed: 'If you stay in here too long, you don't think of guys at all. You just get out of the habit.' The opening siren also echoes the culture's urgent desire to cordon off these tarnished women as quickly as possible, as if their presence in what the film calls 'freeside' could infect the rest of society.

In earlier prison movies featuring men, incarceration is retributive and prohibitive of further crime. In *Caged*, the women are isolated from society not merely as a matter of punishment, but as a matter of public safety explicitly connected to public health. The theme of contagion is introduced early in the film. When a returning prisoner shakes the hand of an inmate scrubbing the floor, the inmate quickly dips her hand in water and wipes it on her shirt. Offended, the new prisoner says: 'Aw, no guy's given me a tumble in months.' During Marie's physical, the nurse complains: 'Hope your batch is cleaner than the last lot. We had to scrub them with brooms.' In order to make sure Marie does not infect the general population, she is placed in isolation for two weeks until her blood test comes back clean. Even her unborn baby is viewed as both a parasitic burden and an infection. 'Another bill for the state', comments the nurse when she learns that Marie is pregnant and her husband is dead. Significantly, the first job Marie is given is to scrub the floor, but the film makes clear that no matter how hard she scrubs, any environment she occupies will remain unclean.

When a group of upper-class welfare women visit the prison, one of them comments: 'It smells like a zoo.' As viewers, we're critical of the woman's callousness, but not necessarily her judgement. Our sympathies remain with Marie, but on the whole, the women's sinful behaviours and carnal appetites are presented as a disease that threatens the larger moral order.

No character embodies that threat more than Harper. As Estelle Freedman points out about post-World War II women's prison films, 'In contrast to the earliest women's prison films, in which the lesbian was portrayed as comic and benign, a dangerously aggressive lesbian criminal now threatened the innocence of young women' (1996: 404). Harper is the film's true menace and primary predator. Although Marie is propositioned by both Kitty and Elvira, neither woman is violent toward her. The choice of sexual involvement is left to her. Elvira, for example, makes it clear she's interested in Marie 'any time you change your type'. Harper, however, uses her position of power and imposing physical size to force herself on Marie. She begins grooming Marie early on, as when she calls Marie into her room while reading *Midnight Romance*, saying: 'Let's you and me get acquainted, honey. You may be a number to the others, but not to me.' Harper's connections to politicians and the criminal underworld allow her to do favours for 'her girls', such as providing drugs and delivering messages to relatives. When Marie tells her she doesn't have any money to pay for such favours, Harper's leers make it clear that the only capital Marie has left is her body, a circumstance that anticipates her final dilemma about how to survive on the ironically named 'freeside'. Kitty and Elvira's advances toward Marie identify them as lesbians, but they retain enough traditional femininity to seem less harmful than Harper, whose overtly butch appearance marks her as an aggressive deviant. The masculinised lesbian of the 1950s, with her erotic independence and defiant rejection of traditional gender roles, has now become the ironic enemy of patriarchy. As such, she is a threat to America itself.

Harper's threat to the American way is further underscored by her close connections to powerful and corrupt government officials. Just as the House Un-American Activities Committee and Joseph McCarthy were rooting out high-ranking communist subversives, so too does the film expose Harper as a dangerous political infiltrator who needs to be destroyed. When Marie refuses to give up her kitten, she does more than defy Harper's order. She defies her identity, revealing herself to be all that

Fig. 9: Harper 'getting acquainted' with Marie in *Caged*.

Harper is not: feminine, maternal, empathetic and nurturing. By cutting Marie's hair in retaliation (an act of symbolic rape), Harper strips her of her femininity, masculinises her appearance and threatens to flip her sexual identity. Though Marie 'toughens up' after the event, her heterosexuality is ultimately validated to viewers by her decision to become a high-end prostitute. As Ann Ciasullo writes, 'the prison lesbian, by representing the threat of contagion, perversion, and permanent inversion, makes possible the patriarchal, heterosexual intervention represented by the male characters' (2008: 218). Even though prostitution is shown to be a tragic end for Marie, it places her in the heterosexual order, making her pimps her rescuers, not from crime, but from the greater atrocity of homosexuality. By the film's end, Harper's death at the hands of Kitty seems both an act of justice and patriotism. Her death also fortifies 'the promise of the prison walls themselves', reassuring viewers that 'the bars and concrete [can] literally contain "deviance," time and time again' (ibid.).

Although it's difficult to find much optimism in *Caged*'s 'good girl turned bad' narrative, the tireless efforts of Warden Benton to bring about reforms provide a modicum of hope, making her the film's genuine hero. Benton's character was actually based on Miriam Van Waters, a liberal reformer who served as the superintendent of the Massachusetts Reformatory for women from 1932 to 1957. As Suzanne Bouchlin describes, Van Waters 'pushed for spiritual guidance, social services, and "maternal love" in place of punishment in women's prisons. She especially strove to instil in women the values of self-sufficiency through paid employment' (2009: 29). Like many film wardens before her, Benton rails against the lack of political will to bring about reform. Her repeated requests for teachers, psychiatrists and better medical facilities are rejected out of hand. When a volunteer doctor contacts the lieutenant governor's office to complain about conditions at the prison infirmary ('When my dog had distemper, I took him to a cleaner infirmary than this one!'), Benton tells a representative of the office: 'I warned you that something like this would happen when the board voted us $8,000 instead of $80,000.' The representative's reply is predictably callous: 'What do you want for your girls now, a swimming pool, television sets, a beauty parlour?' Though Benton is thoroughly dismissed, she reminds the representative that she did get such reforms passed in other institutions, providing evidence to viewers that such changes are possible with political will. Typical of the social problem film, the movie's plea is first and foremost to viewers, calling upon them to notice and care. At one point, Benton flatly states: 'I wish we could drag the public in here to watch the inmates decay.'

It is Marie, however, that viewers truly care about. Although Marie's fate is tragic, Bouchlin finds the ending ambiguous. Benton recognises problems with the system, but she essentially blames Marie's plight on her own moral failings, telling her she needs to have some 'self-respect' and 'decency'. Marie's response ('Where did those things get me, anyway?') reveals 'that those are values that she has always held ... and that the prison system's agents are ill-equipped to impart such ethical guidelines in any event' (2009: 30). Rather than playing the victim, Marie judges the system and reveals *its* moral failures. Benton's efforts, while well intended, 'remain rooted in white middle-class assumptions that particular women (working-class women and, while not cinematically rendered in *Caged*, racialized women) need "help" to "become upright citizens"' (2009: 29). Marie is not a helpless victim at the film's end; rather, she takes her fate in her own hands and makes the best of a system that forms criminals rather than re-forms them.

## Psychologies and pathologies

When *Women's Prison* was released in 1955, the staff reviewer for the *New York Times* dismissed it as a cliché-ridden, 'pat' tale told by 'Hollywood-style penologists' (Anon. 1955). By the mid-1950s, the prison genre had become so familiar to audiences that *Women's Prison* was even able to incorporate a wry meta-commentary about prison movies themselves. A guard's passing comment that she likes to go to prison pictures to 'pick out the flaws' is an amusing admission by the producers that Hollywood has never really gotten prison right. It's also a clever way for the film to dismiss the criterion of 'realism' so often applied by critics to judge the hardboiled prison films of the 1930s. By inoculating itself against the charge of artificiality, *Women's Prison* is able to eschew realism in favour of psychological expressionism. Even the film's opening voice-over, over an exterior shot of the prison, sounds like a therapist examining the unconscious drives of an individual: 'States prison. All prisons look alike from the outside, but inside, each has a different character.' Like many prison pictures, *Women's Prison* ostensibly narrows in on a central issue in need of reform. The voice-over continues: 'In this one, caged men are separated only by a thick wall, from caged women. The system is wrong. But it goes on and on and on. Men and women behind the same walls with only concrete and rifle bullets trying to keep them apart.' Although the warden complains (in typical prison movie fashion) that the state won't budget enough money to build separate institutions, the only people really bothered by the situation are the female superintendent, Amelia van Zandt (Ida Lupino), and the male warden, Warden Brock (Barry Kelley). Throughout the movie, both come across as hyper-strict parents trying to keep their hormone-driven teenagers from sneaking out at night. Like *Caged*, *Women's Prison* employs camp in a way that makes it difficult to pin down exactly what it's saying about sex, borders and the regulation of desire; but what's clear is that it's a far more complex film than the *New York Times* critic gave it credit for.

One of the things that makes *Women's Prison* fascinating is its deconstruction of binaries. The film begins with the induction of two prisoners: Helene (Phyllis Thaxter), a middle-aged housewife who accidentally killed a girl in a car accident, and Brenda (Jan Sterling), a repeat offender returning on a parole violation. From the outset, the film presents the two familiar images of women in the 1950s: the lady and the tramp. Helene, conservatively dressed in a high-collared suit, stands out in sharp contrast to Brenda, whose platinum hair and plunging neckline code her as a prostitute. Unlike most of the 'loose' women in *Caged*, however, Brenda is straight and likeable from the beginning, showing Helene the ropes and acting as her guide. Helene too is a sympathetic character, but not one the viewer can easily identify with for very long. On her first night alone in quarantine, Helene suffers a mental breakdown. She is then placed in a straightjacket and put in a padded cell by the sadistic, emotionally repressed van Zandt, who takes pleasure in torturing the women. Her antagonist, Dr. Crane (Howard Duff) diagnoses her during an argument:

| | |
|---|---|
| Van Zandt: | You know I'm a student of psychology, Doctor. |
| Dr. Crane: | So am I. May I tell you what's wrong with you? |
| Van Zandt: | Do, by all means. |
| Dr. Crane: | You dislike most of the women here because, deep down, you're jealous of them. |
| Van Zandt: | That's absurd. |
| Dr. Crane: | You're feminine, attractive, you must have had opportunities to marry. Maybe you even cared for somebody once in your cold way. |
| Van Zandt: | How dare you! |
| Dr. Crane: | But possibly he turned to somebody who could give him what he really wanted. Warmth, understanding, love. There's hardly a woman inside these walls that doesn't know what love is. |
| Van Zandt: | Yes, and that's why most of them are here. |
| Dr. Crane: | Exactly. Even the broken wrecks have known some kind of love. And that's why you hate them. |

When Dr. Crane discovers what van Zandt has done to Helene, he tells her that Helene is 'suffering from a guilt complex that's close to madness' and admonishes her for putting Helene's life in jeopardy by treating her as a hardened criminal. Van Zandt counters, with no evidence whatsoever, that Helene is a 'borderline psychopath' and must be treated like everyone else. Exacerbating matters, Helene is tortured by not being able to see her devoted husband or read his letters until her thirty-day quarantine period is over. In short, Helene is too frail, too dependent and too lovelorn for

Fig. 10: The naïve Helene and experienced Brenda being inducted in *Women's Prison*.

viewers to identify with for very long, which is why the narrative shifts to the more experienced Joan (Audrey Totter), a fellow prisoner who occupies a space between the 'good girl/bad girl' binary.

Like Helene, Joan is unable to see her husband, Glen (Warren Stevens), not because she is in quarantine but because he is housed on the men's side of the prison. Glen, however, finds a pathway through the wall and manages to visit Joan during her work detail in the laundry. When the good-natured Brenda discovers them in a closet, she sacrifices herself, intentionally scalding her hand in a press to divert the attention of a suspicious matron. Glen and Joan's visit goes undetected, but weeks later, when Joan faints in the laundry, she is forced to reveal that she's pregnant. Furious, Warden Brock demands van Zandt do whatever it takes to get Joan to reveal how Glen managed to get to the women's side, telling her she will be fired if she fails. Joan, who has no idea how Glen managed to make it across, is interrogated and beaten night after night by van Zandt, who eventually goes too far. Glen makes it across one more time, only to find Joan on her deathbed in the infirmary. Upon hearing of Joan's death, the women, led by Brenda, begin to riot as Glen goes on a vengeful rampage with a gun, looking for van Zandt, who he eventually finds hiding in one of the padded cells. His attempt to shoot her, however, is thwarted by Dr. Crane. Having gone mad from fear and emotional repression, van Zandt begins telling Glen she'll get even with him by denying his wife, whom she knows she killed, parole. Dr. Crane explains, 'Don't you see, her mind is gone.' He then orders she be put in a straightjacket. The film ends with the certain resignation of Warden Brock and the release of Helene to her husband's arms.

Above all, *Women's Prison* is a meditation on psychological borders and their permeability. The film sets up numerous binaries and parallels, establishing the tenuous nature of boundaries from the outset by discussing the wall that separates the men from the women. Whereas walls in most prison movies are the obstacles of freedom, walls in *Women's Prison* are the obstacles of Eros, a drive so strong that 'concrete and rifle bullets' can't contain it. Procreation poses more of a threat than liberation to the ruthless and loveless Brock and van Zandt, the cultural curators of desire. Their look of horror when Dr. Crane strolls into Brock's office and says, 'Congratulations, Warden, you two are going to have a baby' reveals not just their fear of losing their jobs but their fear of intimacy. Rather than quietly concealing the pregnancy from higher authorities, they obsess on filling the hole in the wall, an apt metaphor for their sexual repression. When their efforts fail, van Zandt resorts to destroying both Glen's object and product of desire, Joan and the baby. Significantly, the only other person who takes the life of a child in the film is Helene, who comes across as van Zandt's opposite and double. When van Zandt calls Helene a psychopath, Dr. Crane replies: 'You're the psychopath, Amelia.' Van Zandt's earlier use of the term 'borderline psychopath' to describe Helene to her husband is telling because it suggests a certain liminal state, as if she could break one way or the other, depending on her treatment by van Zandt. As Helene's husband declares to van Zandt: 'She wasn't when she came here!' When Helene first arrived, she was completely van Zandt's opposite. Helene, as an empath, feels too much grief for the accidental killing of a child, whereas van Zandt, the psychopath, feels nothing. Helene's sensitivity reduces her to near madness, but by the end of the film, van Zandt's cruelty and lack of remorse reveal her for what she is: insane. As van Zandt sits in the exact same padded cell Helene sat in awaiting a straightjacket, it becomes clear that the woman who looked mad is sane, and the woman who looked sane was mad all along.

*Women's Prison* exhibits the anxiety of the era by demonstrating how quickly things can change and cross over to their opposites. At any moment, housewives can become criminals, peace can become violence, nuclear families can become broken homes, and sanity can become insan-

Fig. 11: Superintendent van Zandt and Warden Brock's reaction upon learning they're 'going to have a baby' in *Women's Prison*.

ity. Although the film criticises the strict regulation of desire and behaviour, it ultimately contains those criticisms in a conservative, heteronormative narrative. Unlike *Caged*, which explores the unsteady line between heterosexuality and homosexuality, *Women's Prison* validates straight desire and marriage. There are very few if any same-sex leers or masculinised women in the film. Instead, the women talk in their sleep about men and dream of going on vacation to Hawaii with their husbands. If anything, the film, despite its opening pronouncement, is critical of the institutional wall that divides men from women and tacitly argues for heterosexual conjugal visits. Though children become an issue, there are no babies conceived or born out of wedlock. Both Glen and Helene's husband remain devoted spouses. And lastly, if Helene is too feeling and van Zandt too unfeeling, Dr. Crane, the film's real centre, inhabits the middle ground. Rational and humane, he appears as the exemplar of patriarchal moderation and moral authority throughout the film.

### Mothers and children

Although often described as a remake of *Caged*, *House of Women* shares little in common with the earlier film except for the inclusion of an inmate,

Erica Hayden (Shirley Knight), who arrives five months pregnant and struggles with the system to keep her baby. After violently resisting her entry into the institution, Erica tells the prison doctor, Dr. Conrad (Jason Evers), that she'd rather lose the baby than have it be born behind bars. In response, Conrad directs her attention to the yard where several inmates are playing with their young children on playground equipment. The inmates, he tells her, are allowed to keep their babies until they are three years old. After that, they will be handed over to the inmate's friends or family members or placed up for adoption if no suitable home can be found. Sentenced to five years for accessory to robbery, Erica is eligible for parole in three years. Because the father was killed during the robbery, the central tension of the film involves Erica's attempt to win parole in time to keep her child.

One of the things that makes *House of Women* unique is its depiction of children behind bars. Ordinary moments of toddlers playing on see-saws and quarrelling over teddy bears are counteracted by disturbing images of children cowering in fear as their mothers attack guards during a riot. Any illusions of domestic bliss are repeatedly shattered by moments of physical and emotional violence. The practice of allowing incarcerated mothers to keep their children for a limited amount of time was nothing new when the film came out. Prison nurseries began at the Bedford Hills Correctional Facility for Women in 1901. Women who gave birth while imprisoned could keep their babies for a year to eighteen months. The arrangement, according to psychologists and penologists, was good for both the child and the inmate. During the early and mid-part of the century, such programmes slowly spread to a limited number of institutions. By the 1960s and 1970s, however, the movement to remove nurseries from prisons gained steady traction, culminating in the publication of an influential 1978 study entitled *Why Punish the Children? A Study of Children of Women Prisoners*, which concluded that, for many children, being raised in a prison 'may be a very traumatic experience with severe negative consequences in terms of their development and future well-being' (quoted in Bloom and Steinhart 1993: 18). Although *House of Women* shows startling images of children being raised in prison, it never really engages in the debates surrounding the morality or effectiveness of such programmes. Already on the wane and studied by only a handful of professionals, prison nurseries were hardly an issue of great public concern. What was of great interest to the general public, however, was child care.

Produced in 1962, *House of Women* arrived in theatres at a time when an increasing number of women were entering the workforce and a growing number of voices were advocating for federal assistance in the raising of children. During the 1960 National Conference on the Day Care of Children in Washington DC, for example, president-elect Kennedy sent a message saying:

> I believe we must take further steps to encourage day care programs that will protect our children and provide them with a basis for a full life in later years. The suggestion of a program of research, financing, and development to serve the children of working mothers and of parents who for one reason or another cannot provide adequate care during the day deserves our full support. (Quoted in Michel 1999: 235)

In 1962 and 1965, Public Welfare Amendments were passed which stipulated that parents should not be allowed to receive child care benefits unless there was a real need, 'broadly construed to mean having a mother who worked, no matter what her income level' (Michel 1999: 243). Though the amendments did provide money for day care, they were actually an attempt to reduce overall welfare payments by requiring women to work or enroll in job training programmes to receive the benefit. The highly contentious issue of child care – of who should provide it, who should pay for it, and what strings should be attached to it – is one that appears in subtle and not-so-subtle ways throughout *House of Women*.

After Erica's arrival, the film jumps forward three years to a cafeteria scene, where the children eat with their mothers and other inmates. After lunch, the mothers drop their children off to the nursery where the matrons watch over them so that the mothers can continue their 'jobs' of being inmates. As Erica places her daughter in her crib, she says: 'You have a good nap and I'll see you at supper', revealing that the matrons watch over the children for the majority of the day. Moments later, Erica and the other women are shown playing baseball in the yard, appearing to enjoy the break from their children. When their recreational time is over, the women proceed to the shop, where they spend the rest of the day sewing uniforms. In the evening, the children are returned to their mothers in the communal cell block. It is a world made up of working mothers, stay at 'home' moms, extended 'family' and friends, and state-funded child care providers, all working in tandem to help raise the children. In any other context, the arrangement might be viewed as one that affords working mothers a healthy balance of quality time with their children, socialisation with other women, and financial independence through honest labour. In the context of prison, however, it seems a perverse parody of what many women were striving for in actuality.

A challenge to the harmonious system arrives in the form of the new warden, Frank Cole (Andrew Duggan). During a meeting with the doctor and the assistant warden, Zoe Stoughton (Margaret Hayes), Cole goes over the expenses and complains first about the milk bill. When the doctor explains that the milk is for the babies, Cole states: 'If I had my way they wouldn't be here', deeming them both an undue burden on the state and a luxury the women shouldn't be allowed. In order to cut costs, he orders that the lights be turned off a half an hour earlier, altering the working rhythm of the inmates' daily lives. When Conrad informs him that the previous warden felt 'the welfare of the inmates was more important than a few dollars', Cole scoffs at the notion of welfare for 'pickpockets, check kiters, blackmailers, drunks, prostitutes, hop-heads', all of whom he considers subhuman. Cole's misogyny stems from his former wife, who recently convinced him to parole an inmate only so that she could run off with him. Now the head of a female institution, Cole has the power to punish all women by denying them benefits and access to their children.

When person after person refuses to accept Erica's baby, Cole has her taken away, without Erica's knowledge, minutes before the child's third birthday party. In protest, Erica's friend, Sophie (Constance Ford), starts a riot, which causes Erica to collapse. While in the infirmary recovering from a breakdown, Dr. Conrad recommends that she be transferred to a lighter work detail. The warden agrees and has her assigned to his own home where she is to perform domestic duties. On the first morning of her new job, Erica carefully places a rose on Cole's breakfast tray, revealing that she intends to seduce the warden in order to win parole and gain back her daughter. In many ways, she becomes a classic *femme fatale*, using her feminine wiles to get what she wants. The difference, however, is that the viewer's sympathies are entirely with her. Her actions, motivated by motherly devotion, are entirely understandable. When the warden eventually succumbs to her sexual allure and falls in love, he begins making life easier for the other inmates. As rumours of the affair spread, the inmates begin whispering behind Erica's back, but they don't outright ostracise her; rather, they remain in relative solidarity, understanding she's doing what she needs to do to get her child back. During the parole hearing, Erica reveals to Cole for the first time that she's secured a job on the east coast and intends to move three thousand miles away with her daughter. During deliberations, the women on the board all agree with Stoughton's senti-ment when she says, 'What's better for a child than to be with its mother?' The wounded Cole, however, convinces the board it would be in the best interest of the child to deny Erica parole and have the girl be adopted by a 'well-established family'. Though his argument is motivated by spite, he successfully makes that case that Erica cannot both work and take care of her baby. He argues that she won't have enough support to succeed because she won't be under the supervision of the parole board. In an earlier parole board hearing, however, one of the other inmates, Candy (Barbara Nichols), refuses her early release, telling the board that the state's 'gift' of parole has 'so many "don'ts" attached to it, you're licked before you start'. After detailing the many bureaucratic strings attached to her release in the past, she concludes: 'Me, I've had it. And believe me it stinks.' The two parole board scenes clearly indicate that any 'benefit' from the state is both burdensome and ineffectual.

Fig. 12: Inmates planning for Erica's daughter's birthday party in *House of Women*.

Like many prison movies, *House of Women* is successful at showing the failures of the system, but fails to offer any solutions. After Candy gives her compelling speech to a rapt parole board, one of the women merely replies: 'You know, I think she's got something' before the scene dissolves. Rather than wrestle with the thorny issues of state support, the film promotes the easy argument implied in Zoe Stoughton's question: 'What's better for a child than to be with its mother?' Following Erica's hearing, the vengeful Cole decrees that all children must be housed in a separate dormitory, where the mothers will only be allowed to visit on Sunday afternoons. In an earlier scene, Sophie is released from solitary and goes to the dormitory to claim her son. When she arrives, however, her son is missing, having crawled out the window in pursuit of a cat while the inmate in charge was sleeping. Sophie stops the boy on the stairs before he can make it to the roof, but scolds the woman in charge, warning her to stay awake next time. She then puts the boy on her back and tells him they're going 'home' before returning to the cell block. The scene is a clear indication that child care outside the 'home', away from a mother's careful supervision, is a danger. The scene is later repeated when the children are forced to stay in the dormitory. Once again, the boy crawls out the window while the supervisor is distracted. This time, however, he makes it to the roof and starts chasing the cat on the ledge. Confined to her cellblock, Sophie can only watch in horror from the window as her son plunges to his death. After suffering a breakdown, Sophie leads a riot, capturing the guards by threatening to gouge their eyes out with knitting needles. When the Director of Corrections, Richard Dunn (Paul Lambert), arrives, the women give their list of demands: parole Erica and give her custody of her child, enact no retaliation against the prisoners, and fire Cole for sleeping with the inmates. All of the demands are eventually granted, and the film ends with Erica embracing her daughter after her release.

As Anne Morey points out, in women's prison films the job of the prison is to act 'as an agent to return women to domesticity' (1995: 80). The presence of children within the prison, however, allows the women to demonstrate their domestic abilities while still incarcerated. All of the mothers in *House of Women* seem innately loving and fiercely protective of their children. If the institution can take any credit for their domestic success, it seems due to the balanced support network displayed in the early part of the film. After Cole's departure, that system may very well be restored by the new warden, Zoe Stoughton. As for Erica, however, she is left on her own, burdened by the parole system, to survive as a working mother. The upbeat ending venerates motherhood, but it also suggests women have an easier time raising children while incarcerated than while 'liberated'.

## Media and morality

Robert Wise's *I Want to Live!* begins with a burst of sound and ends in silence, an apt trajectory for the dramatic life of Barbara Graham, a mother, prostitute and convicted perjurer sent to the gas chamber in 1955 for the murder of a 64-year-old widow named Mabel Monohan. Though the film's opening statement by Pulitzer Prize-winning reporter Edward S. Montgomery states that the film is a 'FACTUAL STORY' of Graham's life, the movie takes a great many liberties. It portrays Graham as a sympathetic figure whose tragic life was largely the consequence of a harsh environment that led her to make a series of reckless and desperate decisions. Graham's complicity in the death of Mabel Monohan is debated to this day, but Wise's film clearly comes down on the side of innocence, depicting an imperfect woman who became the scapegoat for a murder she didn't commit. Despite its deviations from the reality, *I Want to Live!* is a compelling indictment of both the media and the disturbing realities of the death penalty in the 1950s.

The film's opening shot is of a jazz club ceiling, the meaning of which only becomes clear at the end of the introductory sequence. The camera tilts down to a stage where a band plays in propulsive rhythms. A series of canted angles reveal a room full of jazz-loving, hard-drinking, pot-smoking patrons. The camera then moves to the exterior of the building and slowly tilts upward to the room above the bar. As the camera cuts to the interior of the dark room, a silhouetted Barbara Graham (played by Susan Hayward, who won the Academy Award for Best Actress for the role) sits up in bed, lights a cigarette and hands it to the man next to her. It's the room directly above the ceiling in the opening shot. With a Neon 'H' from the hotel sign blazing in the window and smoke filling the room, the shot suggests Barbara Graham has been sitting atop hell all along. Minutes later, a detective enters the room and attempts to arrest the john under the Mann Act, the federal crime of taking a woman across state lines for 'immoral pur-

Fig. 13: Barbara Graham atop hell in *I Want to Live!*.

poses'. Graham, who moments earlier saw a photo of the man's family in his wallet, sacrifices herself, telling the officer that she's the one paying for the room. When the officer asks her if she realises she'll be charged with prostitution, she replies: 'Yeah, I know, and it's a misdemeanor, no federal rap. I've been there before.' As she's being led away, the grateful man says: 'Gee, life's a funny thing', to which Graham responds: 'Compared to what?' The scene cuts directly to a photograph of Graham and a fellow prostitute behind bars, in prison stripes, being courted by sailors.

The opening functions as a microcosm for the entire the film, as time and time again Graham gets embroiled with seedy men in unsavoury situations, takes the brunt of the punishment, and gets transformed into a media representation that fails to tell the whole story. The photograph reveals nothing of her sacrifice for the sake of the man's family; it only conveys the image of a floozy, locked up where she belongs. The film's scrutiny of media's role in shaping public opinion and influencing legal outcomes set it apart from other women's prison films. Sensationalism in journalism is nothing new, of course; nor is its examination by Hollywood, as in *Citizen Kane* (1941). But the rapid expansion of television in the 1950s added a new dimension to media's influence. At the beginning of the decade, there were approximately seven million TVs sold in the US. By decade's end, however, 'Nearly 90 per cent of homes had a TV set' (Halliwell 2007: 147). In addition, advertising and public relations companies began making their presence felt in television, print and radio, leading to a new consumer culture that bought and sold ideas as much as products. *I Want to Live!* portrays Barbara Graham as just another product, one callously created by the media to drive consumption, even to the point of promoting her death.

The first half of the film chronicles Graham's various criminal activities, her gambling and incarceration for perjury, as well as her marriage to a junky, with whom she has a child. Her entanglement with two of her husband's associates, Emmett Perkins (Philip Coolidge) and Jack Santo (Lou Krugman), eventually becomes her undoing when they murder Monohan. In a lengthy sequence, the police trail Graham to a machine shop where Perkins and Santo are hiding. Before surrendering, Santo beats Graham, accusing her of setting the two men up. When it is Graham's turn to emerge from the shop, she pauses in front of a mirror and combs her hair, self-aware that she'll be object of media scrutiny. Upon her surrender, she is greeted by scores of onlookers, mostly teenagers, eating hot dogs and drinking soda, as if watching a movie. She is first approached by the reporter, Ed Montgomery (Simon Oakland), who entreaties: 'Give me a statement and I'll write your angle.' Graham, holding her boy's stuffed tiger, shows her contempt for the press by purring at Montgomery just as a photograph is snapped. The immediate shot afterward is of the photograph, showing Graham snarling at the camera. As soon as Montgomery sees the photo in the darkroom he says to the photographer, 'That's the one to print. "Bloody Babs, the Tiger Woman!"' With that image and label, Graham's fate is largely sealed.

When Graham refuses to testify against Emmett and Santos, they pin the murder on her, leading to a lengthy trial followed closely by the press. The film shows newspaper headlines and radio stations covering the trial in sensationalistic fashion, but its repeated shots of actual television newsman, George Putnam, commenting on the trial highlight the new medium's complicity in Graham's fate. After her inevitable conviction and death sentence, Graham turns her anger toward Montgomery when asked for a statement: 'I want to thank the gentlemen of the press. You chewed me up in your headlines and all the jury had to do was spit me out. You're all invited to the execution. That's only fair. You led the pack, Montgomery. Bring your wife, she'll enjoy it. For once, how about a statement from you. Are you satisfied now!'

Fig. 14: Barbara Graham in the gas chamber, a spectacle to the end.

The second half of the film pursues the question, if the press is powerful enough to get a woman sentenced to death, is it powerful enough to reverse the decision? Dogged by a guilty conscience, Montgomery begins writing sympathetic pieces about Graham, focusing on her difficult upbringing and struggles to raise her child. He then teams with a lawyer and psychologist to sway the courts. After losing appeal after appeal, however, Graham is moved to San Quentin's death row, where even more attempts to stay the execution are attempted. Deadline after deadline are delayed, causing Graham to break down several times. The film doesn't dwell on the legal manoeuvrings, however, focusing instead on Graham and the psychological torture she endures while waiting to be put to death. In stark contrast to the highly stylised opening, Wise employs an unassuming, almost documentary-like tone for the final act of the film. It eschews legal procedural for death procedural, showing men carefully wrapping cyanide eggs in gauze, pouring chemicals in vials, and testing the airlocks of the chamber. When Graham's time is finally up, she asks for a mask so she doesn't have to see the media staring at her through the chamber windows. It also denies the press a complete view of her, a move that mirrors the incomplete way she's been portrayed by them from the beginning.

When Billy Wilder made *Double Indemnity* in 1944, he shot a final scene of murderer Walter Neff (Fred MacMurray) being placed in the gas chamber. He later decided not to use it, both because the film didn't need it and because the censorship office found the image too grotesque. *I Want to Live!*, however, is unflinching in its conviction to show what happens. The gas chamber scene is agonising in its silence and slowness. As Graham sits strapped in a chair, sounds of valves turning and levers being pulled punctuate the silence, demonstrating the terrifying acoustics of extermination. Viewers move in and out of the chamber as Graham waits for something to happen, then struggles to breathe as the gas begins to rise. When the execution is finally complete, Montgomery, who wears a hearing aid, walks out of the prison near the word 'Stop' written on the road. When the rest of the press begin honking their horns in an effort to get their accounts of the execution to their editors first, Montgomery turns off his hearing aid in disgust, and the screen goes completely silent. Disturbingly, the depraved crowd that thrilled to the frenetic jazz at the beginning of the picture have given way to a more 'civilised' general public entertained by the quiet execution of a woman it dubbed 'Bloody Babs'.

Overall, the women's prison films of the 1950s and early 1960s added a psychological dimension to the genre not found in the majority of prison films prior to this period. Although they've often been dismissed as trivial, they actually explore complex issues of gender and morality in an era when such things were difficult to challenge. It's ironic that these thoughtful films, typically targeted to women, became the fodder for the male-oriented women-in-prison sexploitation films of the 1970s and 1980s, such as *The Big Doll House* (1971), *The Big Bird Cage* (1972), *Black Mama, White Mama* (1972) and *Chained Heat* (1983). Such films, often set in exotic locations, pander to a straight male audience by playing up the elements of sadism, voyeurism and submission found in the films of the 1950s and 1960s. Though fascinating in their own right for a host of reasons, women-in-prison films project fantasies. Women's prison movies, however, explore very real anxieties.

## 3    IDENTITY AND VIOLENCE IN POPULAR PRISON FILMS
FROM THE 1960s TO THE 1990s

'It's simple in here. It's an insane place with insane rules, so it
ends up being logical.'

*An Innocent Man* (1989)

In an early scene in Peter Yates's *An Innocent Man* (1989), Jimmie Rainwood
(Tom Selleck) helps his wife prepare for a biology exam by asking her to
define the theory of 'punctuated equilibrium'. The theory, we learn, is that
'evolution is not a series of steady, gradual changes, but is punctuated
by sudden drastic ones'. It is a theory that the rest of the film bears out,
as a string of dramatic events transform the mild-mannered, middle-class
Jimmie Rainwood into Jimmie Rain, the streetwise, hardened prisoner and
ex-con. The beginning of the film shows Jimmie's life running smoothly.
He's got a beautiful wife, a charming home and an ideal job as a maintenance supervisor for American Airlines. His ability to instantly diagnose
a mechanical problem earns him the undying respect and loyalty of his
crew. When an anxious bureaucrat shows up in the hanger to insist that
a plane be ready on time, one of Rainwood's men replies: 'You can't rush
him, Woznick, he's an artist.' Rainwood's steady command of the situation
eventually calms the man down. After Woznick leaves, his crewmate says
sarcastically: 'I really admire that man', to which Rainwood replies: 'Yeah,
he's a great American, Albert.' The men's ridicule of the boss indicates that

it's Rainwood who is the truly great American: hardworking, dedicated and honest. When Rainwood delivers the red, white and blue airplane on time, it's clear he's not only a great American employee, he's a great American citizen.

Though it's never addressed in the film's exposition, central to Rainwood's status as ideal citizen is that fact that he also happens to be white. As Richard Dyer points out, in Western culture, white is almost always an invisible category. In American films, white people are typically portrayed as just people, whereas non-white people are 'raced'. Of this phenomenon, he argues, 'There is no more powerful position than that of being "just" human. The claim to power is the claim to speak for the commonality of humanity' (1997: 2). For the majority of viewers, Jimmie Rainwood represents just such a norm. Had the film gone on to deal with troubles in the marriage or the challenges of raising kids in the suburbs of Los Angeles, Rainwood's race would remain completely unaddressed. Instead, two corrupt cops accidentally break into Rainwood's house, thinking he's a drug dealer. After one of the cops shoots him, mistaking his hairdryer for a gun, the two officers cover up their blunder by planting drugs in the house and placing a fired pistol in Rainwood's hand. When he is eventually convicted and sentenced to six years in a maximum-security prison, his race gradually becomes more noticeable, and the moment he sets foot in the largely-black penitentiary, both Rainwood and the audience experience the film's most dramatic instance of punctuated equilibrium: 'suddenly', 'drastically' Rainwood's whiteness becomes visible. As Dyer points out, often times in order to see whiteness, 'whiteness needs to be made strange' (1997: 9). The prison foregrounds Rainwood's racial particularity, turning his privilege into a liability. By having to confront the parts of America he was able to avoid in the suburbs, Rainwood experiences nothing short of a white middle-class nightmare.

The portrayal of prison as hell is made explicitly clear from the outset. During the transfer to the prison, a returning inmate, Robby (Todd Graff), describes Oroville State Prison as a 'nasty shithole', which proves to be true. Oroville is a dark, dungeon-like institution with cramped brick cells stacked on top of each other as far as the eye can see. Upon entry into the prison one of the guards tells the new inmates: 'You give us a hard time, I guarantee you one long stay in hell.' On Rainwood's first day, Robby is stabbed and set on fire in the yard for having stolen ten cartons of smokes during his previous stint. When Rainwood rushes to put out the fire, he's tackled by Virgil Cane (F. Murray Abraham) who tells him: 'You don't stand around to watch a man die, unless you want to spend the next three years in the hole.' The not-so-subtly named Virgil, Dante's guide through hell in *The Inferno*, becomes Rainwood's mentor for the duration of his stay, advising him on how to survive. For Rainwood, if the prison has a devil, it's a menacing, muscle-bound black inmate named Jingles who wants to make Rainwood his 'kid'. After witnessing Jingles' harassment of Rainwood, Virgil explains how things work in prison: 'It's simple in here. It's an insane place with insane rules, so it ends up being logical. If you're white, you hang white, otherwise the niggers eat you alive. You're not listening to me. Civil rights, brotherly love, all that shit, that gets left at the front gate.' As Virgil suggests, any racial hatreds that might be suppressed or hidden on the outside are visible and distilled in prison, making things 'simple'. In an earlier scene, another white prisoner asks Rainwood: 'You gonna show like a white man or what, Rainwood? Those niggers that just took you on, they belong to the Black Guerrilla Family, and that's some nasty old bucks. You got to deal with that situation or everybody in here's gonna know you're a punk.' The bluntness of the film's racial language is a clear rejection of 'political correctness', a term that was just entering the vocabulary in the late 1980s. In order to survive, Rainwood has to get 'real' and abandon any high-minded, liberal notions of tolerance he might have harboured on the outside.

Rainwood's initial reluctance to kill Jingles changes after the gang leader forces him to watch his men rape another white prisoner. As Angela Farmer explains, in the majority of prison narratives, 'Prison may not be perceived as "so bad" but rape ... is represented as "the worst fate"' (2008: 108). In *An Innocent Man*, if being raped is the worst fate (especially during the 1980s AIDS epidemic), being raped by a black man is even worse, something so awful it justifies Rainwood's decision to kill. As well, for audiences accustomed to seeing Tom Selleck play sensitive yet masculine leading men in films like *Three Men and a Baby* (1987) and the long-running TV show *Magnum P.I.* (1980–88), the idea of witnessing his rape on screen would have been utterly unthinkable. Although the murder of Jingles is presented as justifiable, there is no getting around the fact that the film encourages audiences to take pleasure in the killing of a black Other. Instead of seeing Jingles' violation of Rainwood, viewers

Fig. 15: Jimmie Rainwood's showdown with Jingles in *An Innocent Man*.

see the opposite, as Jingles' death is presented as a symbolic rape. When Rainwood approaches him in the bathroom brandishing a phallic white piece of Plexiglas, Jingles says: 'I'm gonna take that piece and fuck you with it, punk.' Rainwood then outmanoeuvres his foe and penetrates his flesh with his weapon, breaking the handle off and leaving the rest in his body. After the murder, Rainwood does ninety days in solitary (the cost of taking a black life) and becomes a hardened man who's allowed to serve out his time in peace, having earned the same respect in prison as he had at American Airlines.

Like many prison movies, *An Innocent Man* reveals how issues of race, class, gender and sexuality are inextricably intertwined with the themes of power and redemption. Early prison films touched on such issues, but as censorship codes started to erode in the 1960s, prison narratives could become much more explicit in their explorations of those themes. Films from *The Defiant Ones* to *The Shawshank Redemption* and beyond have repeatedly confronted the thorny issues of identity, discrimination and violence in ways only the prison genre can. By placing disparate groups of people in stressful, contained spaces, prison movies bring to light the prejudices, fears and anxieties of society as a whole.

*Prison buddy films*

Because prison movies often examine the close bonds between men, it's no surprise that they take on many of the characteristics of 'the buddy film'. Broadly defined,

> Buddy films offer a space for negotiating masculine crises incited by issues of class, race and gender through the juxtaposition of two men of differing personalities and backgrounds and their evolving relationship. These differences are accepted over the course of their adventures as both men recognize that together they can face that which threatens their masculinity – whether women, the enemy, or the law. (Kimmel and Aronson 2004: 113–14)

An enduring genre, the buddy film reaches as far back as Laurel and Hardy in the 1930s to *Butch Cassidy and the Sundance Kid* (1969) in the 1960s, the *Lethal Weapon* films in the 1980s, to the Judd Apatow 'bromances' of the 2000s. As Nicole Rafter points out, one of the answers as to why prison movies appeal 'lies in the films' encouragement of fantasies about sex and rebellion' not sanctioned in everyday life (2006: 172). Prison films have exploited fantasies and the dynamics of 'differing personalities' from their earliest days, but as America experienced Vietnam, Civil Rights and the feminist movement, prison movies began focusing more on the interpersonal relationships between men as a means of examining challenges to patriarchy.

One of the first prison films to directly address the issue of race is Stanley Kramer's 1958 film, *The Defiant Ones*. When a prison transport truck overturns during a rainstorm, chained inmates John 'Joker' Jackson (Tony Curtis) and Noah Cullen (Sidney Poitier) go on the lam in the Southern countryside. The film chronicles their attempts to evade capture by a bloodhound-guided posse of police officers and deputised citizens. The leader of the posse, Sheriff Max Muller (Theodore Bikel), states that he's not terribly concerned about catching the men because, most likely, 'they'll kill each other before they go five miles'. Unlike the vast majority of American action films, *The Defiant Ones* doesn't tell the story of an individual hero defying the odds to accomplish a task. Rather, it places a couple at its centre in the tradition of the romantic comedy, the arc of which is best summed up in a paraphrase of an exchange between Billy Crystal and Meg Ryan in *When Harry Met Sally* (1989): The first time we met we hated each other, then we became friends, and then we fell in love.

A critical and popular success, *The Defiant Ones* won Academy Awards for Best Original Screenplay and Best Black and White Cinematography, and both Poitier and Curtis were nominated for Best Actor. The film's importance and recognition derive from its historical context. As Vera Hernan and Andrew M. Gordon point out, the film 'appeared in the wake of such events as the 1954 Supreme Court decision on school desegregation in *Brown v. Board of Education of Topeka Kansas*, the 1955–56 Montgomery Bus Boycott, and the 1957 use of federal troops to integrate Little Rock's Central High, landmark events that moved the urgent need for racial change to the center of the American consciousness' (2003: 155). The director, Stanley Kramer, made several socially liberal 'message films' throughout his career, including *On the Beach* (1959), *Inherit the Wind* (1960) and *Guess Who's Coming to Dinner* (1967), the last of which also starred Sidney Poitier. In an interview, Kramer made clear his intention in making *The Defiant Ones*: 'It was my purpose to stress the idea about all human beings having basically the same nature. To show this, I took two human beings on the lowest possible level to tell the glory of the sacrifice for a man, to stress the need they have for each other' (quoted in Hernan and Gordon 2008: 156). On the face of it, the film is a parable of race relations in America. Despite the fact that Cullen and Jackson hate each other, they must cooperate in order to survive. At one point, Jackson pulls Cullen out of a raging river. At another, Cullen lets Jackson stand on his shoulders to escape from a clay pit. Neither of these acts are altruistic, of course. Until the two men are able to break the chain that binds their wrists, they need to keep the other alive. As Jackson says after Cullen thanks him for pulling him out of the river: 'Man, I didn't pull you out. I kept you from pulling me in.'

The obviousness of the film's premise is transcended by the strong performances of Curtis and Poitier. At a time when virtually no black actors were offered leading roles, Sidney Poitier occupied a special place in Hollywood. His appeal was universal, but he was self-consciously aware that no matter what role he played, he would be perceived as *the* face of black America. In *The Defiant Ones*, Poitier does an admirable job of making Cullen a complex, three-dimensional character, one imbued with both sensitivity and justifiable hatred. Still, as with the majority of films Poitier made, he was in the hands of white producers, writers and directors who, however well-intended, presented first and foremost the perspective of white liberalism. It's a credit to Poitier's talents that he was able to bring as much individual humanity to his characters as he did. Such humanity surfaces in conversations with Jackson throughout *The Defiant Ones*. Cullen gradually reveals details about his past, informing Jackson that he has a wife and a child who no longer remembers him. After years of his wife telling him to 'be nice' in the face of discrimination, Cullen finally erupted against a white man who came on his property with a gun to collect money. He took the gun away and beat the man to within an inch of his life before he was pulled off. Cullen's anger is clearly earned; Jackson's, however, is absorbed. When Cullen confronts Jackson about calling him a nigger, Jackson states: 'Don't crowd me cuz I didn't make up no names.' Cullen replies: 'No, you breathe it in when you're born and you spit it out from then on.' Jackson insists that everybody has to live by the existing rules, by the natural order, because 'everybody stuck with what he is'. On the face of things, the film argues that both men need to overcome their prejudices, and it suggests the characters need to meet each other half way. The very chain that connects them, however, reveals a false equivalency of forgiveness and identification. It's one thing to see a white man in chains, which marks him as a prisoner, but it's quite another to see a black man in chains, which signifies him as a slave. Much more is asked of Cullen – and of Poitier. As James Baldwin put it, 'the hatred is not equal on both sides, for it does not have the same roots … black men do not have the same reason to hate white men as white men have to hate blacks' (2011: 64).

*The Defiant Ones* claims there can be an identification with others through mutual suffering, but in order to truly understand Cullen's plight, Jackson would have to have experienced generations of endemic prejudice on the same level as Cullen, which is impossible. This becomes most clear when Cullen and Jackson narrowly escape being lynched after breaking into a general store and injuring a white man at a turpentine camp. As he's about to be strung up, Jackson says: 'Don't you understand? You can't go lynching me. I'm a white man!' The situation allows him to experience the same fear thousands of blacks experienced in the past, but any genuine identification is trumped by his incapacity to comprehend what's happening. In his mind, the men at the camp are simply making a mistake. His comment further reveals his belief that it's still acceptable to lynch a black man, a notion not lost on Cullen who gives him a caustic glare. Just as Mack (Claude Akins) is about to string both men up after Cullen spits in his face, Sam (Lon Chaney Jr.) steps forward and defends the men, knocking out Mack in the process. The next morning as Sam surreptitiously cuts Cullen and Jackson loose, the men see a scar on his wrist, revealing that he's spent time on a chain gang himself. When Cullen asks for a crowbar to break the chain, Sam tells him: 'Don't go to pressing your luck too far, boy.' His suffering has fostered empathy, but it has its limits, especially when it comes to Cullen. As he watches the two men run away, he says to himself: 'Run, chicken, run', wishing for their getaway. The singular 'chicken', however, most certainly refers only to Jackson. Sam's limited empathy toward Cullen merely shows strides, making Jackson's recognition of Cullen as an equal by the end of the film seem all the more remarkable. Jackson is exceptional in his capacity to overcome prejudice.

Much discussed is the homosocial bond the two men form throughout the film. The chain, of course, forces the men to be in close physical proximity to each other and touch. In an early scene, Jackson wakes up in the rain only to find himself with his arm wrapped around Cullen, whose head is on his stomach. His look of discomfort comes across as comic, a common move of 'buddy films' to assure viewers – and often the characters themselves – that what they're witnessing is male bonding rather than homosexual desire. At another point, as the men argue about heading north or south, Cullen holds up the chain and tells Jackson: 'You married to me alright, Joker, and here's the ring.' As the men's psychic journey continues, Jackson grows increasingly physically vulnerable. While being lowered into the general store, Jackson cuts his wrist, a wound that eventually becomes infected. The moment the men finally break the chain at the farm of an unnamed woman (played by Cara Williams) where they have taken refuge, Jackson passes out from the infection and Cullen carries him to bed. M. K. Franklin argues that the 'opening up and creation of a wound can be seen as a feminization' (1990: 125). Jackson's vulnerability, his openness, then sparks competition between Cullen and the woman to see who can best take care of him. While Cullen is asleep, the woman seduces Jackson and convinces him to leave Cullen behind and run away with her. When Jackson learns that the woman has sent Cullen off to drown in a dangerous swamp, however, he chases after Cullen, realising his relationship with him is far more valuable and genuine. The woman's treachery and absolute lack of conscience, coupled with Cullen's anger at his wife for demanding he suppress his true feelings, suggest a latent misogyny within the film. It is as if the women have to be demonised in order to justify the men's preference for a homosocial, if not outright homosexual, relationship.

One of the best commentaries on *The Defiant Ones* comes from writer James Baldwin, who wrote about it in his book, *The Devil Finds Work*, first published in 1976. Baldwin took particular issue with the film's ending. When Cullen and Jackson finally reach the train, Cullen jumps aboard and offers his outstretched hand to Jackson, who cannot keep up because of a gunshot wound inflicted by the woman's son. Once it becomes clear that Jackson's not going to make it, Cullen jumps off the train and the two men go rolling down the hill together. At the conclusion, Cullen sings 'Sewing Machine' and cradles Jackson in his arms in the manner of a *pieta* as they wait for the approaching sheriff to take them back into custody. Of the different experiences of the film's audiences, Baldwin writes: 'Liberal white audiences applauded when Sidney, at the end of the film, jumped off the train in order not to abandon his white buddy. The Harlem audience was outraged, and yelled, *Get back on the train, you fool!*' (2011: 65). Baldwin states: 'There is no way to believe both Noah Cullen *and* the story' (2011: 64) because Noah's decision to stay with Jackson rather than seek free-

Fig. 16: Noah Cullen cradling 'Joker' Jackson in the final scene of *The Defiant Ones*.

dom rings false. The motivation for the ending, he argues, comes from somewhere else: 'He jumps off the train in order to reassure white people, to make them know that they are not hated; that, though they have made human errors, they have done nothing for which to be hated' (2011: 68). Others have been critical of the film as well. Emma Hamilton and Troy Saxby, for example, take issue with the film's suggestion that 'the capacity to overcome racism' can best be achieved by 'personal change rather than institutional restructuring' (2011: 78). Regardless of one's take on the film – a film even Baldwin called 'genuinely well-meaning' (2011: 63) – *The Defiant Ones* stands out among other prison pictures precisely because of its racial contradictions and controversies.

In response to the growing conformity of the 1950s, Hollywood began cultivating the figure of the antihero in films like *A Streetcar Named Desire* (1951) and *The Wild One* (1953). By the Vietnam era, the figure of the disillusioned, anti-authoritarian was perfected by Paul Newman as Lucas Jackson in Stuart Rosenberg's *Cool Hand Luke*. The film opens with a drunk Luke circling around a parking meter, cutting its head off as the word 'Violation' flashes on screen – a perfect metaphor for a man spiraling out of control. Sentenced to two years on a Florida chain gang for destroying municipal property, Luke enters into an authoritarian environment completely unconcerned with human rights. Upon his entry into the camp, we learn that Luke is a decorated World War II veteran who rose to the rank of sergeant but who was busted back to private by the time he left. Few details are given about his time in the war, but as the film progresses it becomes clear that his guilt over having killed enemy soldiers is at least a partial catalyst for his self-destructive tendencies. At the end of the film he confesses to God: 'I know I'm a pretty evil fellow.' It's impossible to say that Luke is completely self-destructive, however, because no matter how much trouble he gets himself into, there's also a merciless authoritarianism ready to willfully destroy him. The camp's arbitrary rules and punishments are quickly established by Carr, the floorwalker (Clifton James), on Luke's first day: 'Any man forgets his number spends a night in the box. These here spoons you keep with you. Any man loses his spoon spends a night in the box. There's no playing grab-ass or fighting in the building. You got a grudge against another man, you fight him Saturday afternoon. Any man playing grab-ass or fighting in the building spends a night in the box...' In one of several homages to *I Am a Fugitive from a Chain Gang*, the inmates must ask permission for even the smallest actions, like wiping sweat from their brows and taking off their shirts.

Luke's refusal to conform earns him the increasing wrath of the guards, but also the increasing respect of his all-white fellow inmates. During a lengthy boxing match with Dragline (George Kennedy), Luke refuses to give up even though he takes a brutal pounding. As the fight lingers on, even Dragline tells him to stay down, not wanting to hurt him any more than he already has. By refusing to give up, Luke turns his defeat into a victory and gains an elevated status among the inmates. The men in the camp bond with one another through their mutual adoration of Luke and his tenacity. He becomes almost legendary in their eyes, a projection of what they wish they could be. It would be inaccurate to say that Luke has any real friends in the camp, though all of the inmates think he is theirs. Even as Dragline grows increasingly enamored of Luke, calling him 'my darlin'' and 'my poor baby', Luke remains aloof. His connection to the men is presented as more spiritual than emotional. Christian imagery abounds in the film, particularly in one of the movie's most famous scenes: Luke's bet that he can eat fifty eggs. When Dragline asks him why he couldn't have picked a smaller number like 35 or 39, Luke replies, 'it seemed a nice round number'. The number, however, is not arbitrary, as there are fifty men in the camp. Luke begins to take on the role of a martyr, devouring the sins of each man with every egg. As he struggles to finish number 41, Dragline tells him, 'Just nine more between you and everlasting glory!' At the scene's conclusion, an overhead shot shows Luke displayed on the table like Christ on the

Fig. 17: Luke as Christ on the cross after eating fifty eggs in *Cool Hand Luke*.

crucifix. This act of consummation is later returned as the men help Luke when he is given the punishment of eating an enormous amount of food by the guards.

Luke, however, is an uneasy martyr. While free during a temporary escape, he sends a manufactured photo of himself with two beautiful women back to the camp. The men talk incessantly about Luke and the women to the point where they begin to live vicariously through him. It is as if they are entering Luke in order to fulfill their erotic dreams. In an earlier scene, the men leer at a woman provocatively washing her truck and join in a common fantasy of sleeping with her. Immediately following the scene, the men are shown naked in the shower, still talking about her and turning each other on. Though the men express their longing to sleep with women, each man functions as a stimulus for the others' sexual arousal. In this fashion, the men engage in a homoerotic bond while simultaneously affirming their heterosexuality. In actuality, the woman is as much an imaginary object of gratification as the photo, which Luke placed in a magazine next to an article called 'The Illusion That Kills' with an accompanying picture of man pointing a rifle at the photo. When Luke is returned, battered and beaten, the men crowd around him, again on the table, asking for stories about his adventures with the women. Sick, tired and resentful of their idolatry, he shouts: 'Stop feeding off me!' He even turns away Dragline, whose very name suggests an obstacle dragging him down.

By the film's conclusion, Dragline becomes the film's Judas, leading the police to an abandoned church where Luke is hiding out from another escape. During his conversation with God, Luke says: 'It's beginning to look like You got things fixed so I can't never win out. Inside, outside, all of them ... rules and regulations and bosses.' Fully realising he's been operating in a rigged system, the only thing left for him to do is complete his self-destructive martyrdom. Luke's final words before he's shot are a parroting back of the film's most famous line, spoken to him by the prison captain (played by Strother Martin): 'What we got here is a failure to communicate', signifying Luke's absolute refusal to capitulate to the authoritarian system that the captain and the soulless Boss Godfrey (i.e. godless) represent. Bruce Crowther argues that *Cool Hand Luke* 'depicts a foredoomed life that provides an uplifting message for the central character's fellow inmates and, perhaps, to the wider audience' (1989: 34). It is difficult, however, to see the death of Luke as 'uplifting'. His relentless resistance is indeed life-affirming, but it is also shown to be wholly ineffectual within the world of the film. He is shot primarily so that his independence doesn't spread, which it certainly won't to any of the characters in the film. Though *Cool Hand Luke* never deals directly with issues of race and civil rights, it can perhaps best be understood as a film admiring of the indomitable spirits of the era's very real martyrs.

*Prison and sports*

In *Hollywood from Vietnam to Reagan*, Robin Wood draws attention to the demeaning and marginalised roles provided to women in the buddy films of the 1970s. The numerous depictions of close-knit relationships among men at the expense of women were in part a backlash against feminism's challenge to patriarchy. He notes that 'if women can be dispensed with so easily, a great deal else goes with them, including the central supports of and justification for the dominant ideology: marriage, family, home' (1986: 227). These dismissals, he argues, 'are the direct product of the crisis in ideological confidence generated by Vietnam and subsequently intensified by Watergate' (1986: 228). No film of the 1970s establishes the above tendencies more quickly than Robert Aldrich's *The Longest Yard* (1974) (also known as *The Mean Machine*). The opening shot of the film surveys a living room, decorated with feminine touches, fashion magazines and numerous photos of the home's wealthy owner, Melissa (Anitra Ford). From the bedroom we hear the telecast of a football game and Melissa's voice saying: 'only a moron can sit and watch two football games one after the other'. The scene cuts to a shot of the bedroom where former quarterback, Paul Crew (Burt Reynolds), feigns sleep in order to avoid having sex with Melissa. When she rolls on top of him, he throws her violently to the floor and begins getting dressed to leave. As he gathers his things, she tells him: 'You split when I tell you to split, you All-American son-of-a-bitch.' Soon after she calls him a 'has been' and a 'whore', not only for being a kept man, but also for taking a payoff to shave off points in a game, a decision that cost him his career. When she blocks his path to the door and slaps his face, he slams her against the door, mashes her face with his hand, and throws her forcefully to the ground. It is a disturbingly realistic depiction of domestic violence. 'Home', for Crew, is a place of complete emasculation, and Melissa's repeated attacks on his masculinity encourage his violence

Fig. 18: Paul Crew's startling violence against Melissa at the opening of *The Longest Yard*.

against her. When he peels out the driveway in her Maserati, the tone is one of emancipation. After leading police on a wild chase and dumping the car in the bay, Crew is eventually arrested for theft, drunk driving and resisting arrest. As he enters Citrus State Prison, Crew's actions seem not so much motivated by self-destruction as by a deep desire to renounce everything domestic and return to a world of men.

The *Longest Yard* is first and foremost a prison movie, but in addition to incorporating elements of the buddy film, it is also helped popularise the underdog sports movie, initiating a cycle of films such as *Rocky* (1976), *The Bad News Bears* (1976), *Gus* (1976), *Slap Shot* (1977) and *Breaking Away* (1979). In many ways, Paul Crew is 'Cool Hand' Luke Jackson's antithesis. Whereas Jackson was born a steadfast nonconformist, Crew has been a conformist all his life. As Melissa tells him: 'Everybody's bought you. Colleges, the pros, your gamblers.' The film associates selling out with femininity and makes football the arena in which Crew can gain back – or rather, find – his manhood. David Gonthier argues that Crew's passive watching of football at the beginning spurs his violent actions, putting in motion, however unconsciously, a 'former jock's dream of getting back into the game' (2006: 119). Significantly, both prison and the football field are arenas in which Crew doesn't have to compete with women; they are fantasy spaces that remove any feminine challenges to masculine hierarchies.

Crew's arrival poses an immediate threat to Captain Knauer (Ed Lauter), coach of the prison guards' semi-pro football team. Knauer pulls Crew into his office and beats him with a baton, telling him to turn down the warden's request to help coach the team. When he does so, Warden Hazen (Eddie Albert), makes his life hell to the point where Crew agrees to help – not by coaching, but by putting together a team of inmates so that the guards can have a practice game. A significant portion of *The Longest Yard* concerns Crew's attempts to assemble his team. The majority of inmates are reluctant to sign on, not only because Crew once had it all and threw it away but because, as Caretaker (James Hampton) puts it: 'You could have robbed banks, sold dope, stole your grandmother's pension checks and none of us would have minded. But shaving points off a football game? Man, that's un-American.' After Caretaker's statement, the film's concerns with national identity begin to emerge, as Crew has now been called both 'All-American' and 'Un-American', ideal citizen and fraud. The film suggests that Paul Crew, like America itself, projected an image of himself that was never true. This theme of nationhood is further underscored by the patriotic, yet sadistic Warden Hazen, who wears an American flag pin on his lapel and self-consciously promotes a fictitious image of himself as a patriot. When he spouts his most self-important platitudes about teamwork and character, he makes sure his Assistant Warden (played by Mort Marshall) records the statements for posterity. Similarly, the film's repeated use of the word 'history' highlights the familiar notion that history is a story told from the perspective of the powerful. For Crew to redeem himself, he must exhibit a true image of both himself and America; thus, he must make amends for his (and, by extension, the nation's) past and assemble a multicultural *crew* representative of the real American story.

It is no surprise that the white inmates get over their resentments of Crew fairly quickly, overlooking his past and seizing on the opportunity to take hits on the guards during the actual game. They come to him. It is significant that the first non-white inmate Crew has to recruit is a Native American prisoner named Indian, the representative of a people betrayed time and time again by the American government. By agreeing to join the team, Indian takes his chances and places his trust in a white authority yet again. Crew's attempts to persuade the black players to join the team, however, prove more difficult. During a conversation among the black inmates, one says: 'This honky golden boy sold out his own teammate, didn't he?' He continues: 'He did it once, he'll do it again.' When Crew approaches the black inmates on a basketball quart, they view him with contempt and suspicion. Even though two of the men used to play professional football, they tell him: 'We no longer perform for the honky's amusement', understanding they've served a system that never served them. When one of the older black inmates, Granville (Harry Caesar), agrees to play, the other black inmates begin to view him as an Uncle Tom. Crew's attempt to recruit the rest of the black players does not succeed. It is only after Granville is deliberately humiliated by a white officer in the library that they agree to join the team. Their decision seems motivated as much by a desire to defeat white oppression as by a desire to exhibit solidarity with the older generation of pre-Civil Rights African-Americans Granville represents.

Before the team even steps on the field, Crew is able to gain a tentative loyalty by extending the privileges granted to him by the warden. He gets the inmates better food and keeps them off their work details. The inmates withhold their trust and respect, however, until Crew proves it to them, which he does during practices, exhibiting integrity and the kind of high-minded ideals touted by Warden Hazen earlier in the film. During the actual game, however, Crew cuts a deal with the warden to throw the game in order to avoid serving more time on a false accessory to murder charge. The second half of the game is genuinely painful to watch, as Crew gives up points, feigns injury, and lets down teammate after teammate. Crew's breaking point comes when he's approached by Granville, the film's true moral conscience. He tells Crew: 'You fooled the hell out of me. I put my trust in you, and you let me down like this. Look, I know you don't give a shit about nothin', but I didn't think you'd sell us out.' Moments later, after Granville is injured and taken off the field, a guilt-stricken Crew asks the paternal Pop if it was worth doing an extra thirty years for slugging Hazen in the mouth years ago. Pop replies, 'for me it was'. The instant Crew changes his mind and decides to sacrifice himself for his team, a red, white and blue banner is shown over his shoulder. The no-longer fictitious All-American, stand-up guy then rejoins the team, builds back their trust, and eventually wins the game.

By defeating the guards, the Mean Machine alter the fictitious script created by Warden Hazen. It is for this reason that the Assistant Warden,

Fig. 19: Paul Crew's All-American moment of truth during the big game.

finally fed up with all of Hazen's oppressive posturing, turns to him in disgust and says, 'His-to-ry', meaning not just that the game is over, but that what everyone has just witnessed was something authentic and out of his control. That authenticity, of course, extends to Crew, who may remain under the control of Hazen for years to come, but who will also serve his time as a real man. *The Longest Yard* may at first glance seem like a frivolous film, but a closer look reveals it to be time capsule of a deeply disillusioned, post-Vietnam, post-Watergate America struggling with gender, race and the difference between idealism and reality.

*The Longest Yard* was not the only prison movie around this time to incorporate sports into its narrative. Jamaa Fanaka's low-budget exploitation movie *Penitentiary* (1979), starring Leon Isaac Kennedy, built its story around boxing tournaments set in an almost exclusively black prison. Similarly, Sidney Poitier, who starred in *The Defiant Ones*, directed *Stir Crazy* (1980), a comedy starring Gene Wilder and Richard Pryor as two wrongfully convicted men who get involved in a prison rodeo. Though neither film is as compelling as *The Longest Yard*, both contribute to the investigation of race, gender and sexuality in prison stories. *Penitentiary*, especially, addresses the issues of prison rape and masculinity head on with its inclusion of an inmate who is repeatedly raped by his cellmate. The film also includes an extended, exhausting fight scene in which one inmate tries to rape another. Set against the backdrops of prison and the world of boxing, the film shows characters attempting to redeem or reclaim their masculinity through the sanctioned violence of the ring. One of the best comments on the film comes from the *New York Times* critic, Vincent Canby, who noted: 'The strongest statement of the film – and one that can't be dismissed – is that 99 per cent of these inmates are black.' *Penitentiary*, though a low-budget, poorly acted film, gave visibility to black incarceration long before black stars appeared as leading protagonists in big-budget prison films.

*Stir Crazy* is a much more light-hearted film that nonetheless contains interesting elements. The inclusion of a rodeo competition with a rival prison is primarily a plot device that allows the prisoners to hatch an escape plan during the film's final act. The rodeo's other reason for being is to illustrate, as in *The Longest Yard*, institutional corruption. Ostensibly an event to raise money for the inmates, the 'Annual Top Hand Rodeo Competition' is actually the occasion for long-running, high-stakes bets between Warden Beatty (Barry Corbin) and his rival warden. One of the inmates reveals that in all the years the rodeo's been running, the prisoners have only received a box of ping-pong balls. Though it doesn't address race directly, it does deal with the dynamics of interracial friendships among a group of prisoners. Notable also is its inclusion of several stereotypical gay characters, types which also appear in *The Longest Yard* and *Penitentiary*. Visibility may be seen as progress, but as Robin Wood points out, outlandish gay characters, rather than being fully realised human beings, 'merely guarantee the heroes' heterosexuality'; gay characters often have 'the function of a disclaimer – our boys are not like that' (1986: 229). More complex gay characters would only appear later in such prison narratives as *Kiss of the Spider Woman* (1985) and HBO's *Oz*.

## Prison and rape

In *Shots in the Mirror*, Nicole Rafter observes that prison films 'encourage sexual reveries through their concern with issues of domination and submission, entrapment and escape, control and powerlessness. Their preoccupation with punishment, cruelty, sadism, hidden enemies, and violation speaks in undertones of sadomasochism to those who might be listening' (2006: 173). Of all of the astute points in that passage, the most salient might be contained in the words 'to those who might be listen-ing'. Although sex in prison films is certainly prevalent, it's also easy to see innuendo in virtually everything, from prison architecture (e.g., the drainpipe in *The Shawshank Redemption*) to character names (e.g., Charlie Butts in *Escape from Alcatraz*) to forms of punishment (e.g., 'the hole' in virtually every prison film). Still, sex in prison films plays an important role, defining power relationships, racial dynamics, gender identity and even love. Because of censorship restrictions, earlier prison films can be fasci-nating for their subtexts and 'codings' of certain characters and situations. The ambiguities of such scenes open up wide ranges of interpretation, of course. In a scene in Jules Dassin's *Brute Force* (1947), for example, a sadistic guard named Munsey (Hume Cronyn) plays Wagner records while savagely beating a prisoner with a club, an act one critic says expresses his Nazism (see Horton 1984: 23) and another says 'expresses his gay-ness' (Dyer 1993: 67) – not that those are mutually exclusive. Films from the 1970s onward, however, are much more direct and explicit.

The one act even the most uninitiated prison film viewer most likely expects to see, or see referenced, is rape. As Angela Farmer writes,

> 'Don't drop your soap in the shower' is cliché advice given to any male sentenced to serve in a general population prison and it reveals an anxiety surrounding anal rape in prison. It is a notion derived from fear rather than veracity. In popular American culture, jokes, sitcoms, and even television commercials indicate that male rape in prison is widespread and prevalent. (2008: 107)

The recent Will Ferrell and Kevin Hart comedy vehicle *Get Hard* (2015) is a testament to Farmer's point, as the film includes so many prison rape jokes as to become tedious at best, homophobic at worst. Despite popular belief, the prevalence of male rape is 'not substantiated by empirical data' (ibid.), which is not to dismiss it as a very real problem. Rather, it goes to show that the presentation of rape as a certainty in prison films is a fantasy that speaks more about the popular culture than prison culture.

Rape scenes often appear early in prison films as key moments that test a character's ability to survive behind bars. The message seems to be that if a character can stave off an initial rape attempt through some demonstration of physical prowess, his masculinity will be affirmed and his time in prison will be bearable. This is certainly the case in *Escape from Alcatraz*. Not surprisingly, the attempted rape scene occurs in the shower and involves soap. Frank Morris (Clint Eastwood) is approached by Wolf (Bruce Fischer), who begins by making small talk and then makes his intentions clear. He states: 'I'm looking for a new partner', to which Morris replies dismissively: 'Good luck'. When Wolf makes it known his proposal isn't optional, Morris punches him repeatedly in the stomach and groin, shoves a bar of soap in his mouth, and kicks him to the floor. As Nicholas Chare points out, the use of soap signals that 'Wolf's actions are to be understood as unclean' (2015: 45). Importantly, Morris pummels Wolf in full view of the guards, who neither stop the fight nor punish Morris afterwards. In almost every prison movie, when a fight breaks out, the guards are quick to act and the warden quick to discipline, especially when it's a new inmate. The guards' inaction, in either preventing the rape or stopping the beating, signify rape as a kind of sanctioned initiation ritual. Immediately after Morris puts Wolf in his place, he is essentially rewarded with a plum job delivering books from the prison library, a job that associates him with knowledge, intellect and movement. It's here that he meets a black inmate and supervisor named English (Paul Benjamin), who asks him: 'You treat them all like Wolf?' Morris replies: 'Wolf wanted to get friendly. I didn't', informing English that his violence was strictly an act of self-defence. English then reveals that he's serving two back-to-back 99-year prison sentences for killing two white men who came at him with knives in an Alabama bar. Morris states: 'Seems like you could have pleaded self-defence', to which English responds: 'The dudes were white, man. Just like you.' In essence, both Morris and English did the same thing by standing up for themselves in the face of a threat. But whereas Morris gains increased control over his body for doing so, English loses control over his, suggesting a type of rape the criminal justice system imposes on him because of his race. When Morris makes his first book delivery, a black inmate asks him: 'What'd they do? Give a nigger a nigger of his own?' Because of an increased mobility gained by asserting power over a rapist, Morris is able to show his superiority to the man stuck in the cell (and by extension, English) by simply walking away.

Unlike Morris, who was a seasoned veteran of the system when he entered Alcatraz, young characters who enter prison (or juvenile hall) are shown to be particularly vulnerable to rape. An early and rather shocking instance of this appears in Willis Goldbeck's 1949 film *Johnny Holiday* (re-released in 1955 as *Boy's Prison*). When a teenage boy re-enters a reform school after an escape attempt, the other boys, who have been punished on his behalf, force him into the showers. Though shot from outside the shower room, the suggestion is clear when one boy after another goes into the room and tosses his towel out the door. When the boy emerges bleeding and doubled-over, he refuses to tell one of the adults what happened to him. In Barry Levinson's *Sleepers* (1996), a group of young boys are repeatedly raped by adult guards at the Wilkinson Home for Boys. Upon their release, the boys decide never to tell anyone about the horrors they endured, agreeing that 'the truth stays with us'. As the film plays out, it becomes clear that the fates of the boys as adults are essentially determined by their ordeals at the reformatory.

A somewhat similar situation occurs in Edward James Olmos's *American Me* (1992). During his first night in juvenile hall, a young Montoya Santana (Panchito Gomez) is raped by an older boy at knifepoint. Unlike the boys in *Sleepers*, however, Santana enacts immediate revenge, grabbing the knife from the boy and stabbing him in the throat as a young onlooker and apparent victim says: 'Kill him, kill him.' The revenge is imperative to Santana's survival and maintenance of masculinity, especially in relation to the macho Chicano culture in which he grows up. In a society where females are thought of as 'passive and receptive, the female body is defined by its capacity to be penetrated; it is violable' (Farmer 2008: 107). Therefore, 'for a man to be raped is for him to be feminized and, in a misogynistic culture, this is a fate worse than death' (ibid.). Even though Santana has been raped, he is able to reclaim his masculinity by penetrating the boy's throat, feminising him with the knife. Rather than suffering further abuse from the other boys, Santana becomes the dominant masculine presence at the facility. Immediately following the killing, he is shown strutting around the grounds to the sound of 'Rockin' Robin' as the other boys look at him with respect. As the voice-over of an adult Santana states: 'Killing that first night got me the worst that juvie had to offer. Extended sentence with a guaranteed bus ride to the big time as soon as I turned eighteen. But the respect I earned made me think I'd found the answer.' Unlike the boys in *Sleepers*, Santana enacts revenge and gains respect, but like them, he finds the rest of his life dictated by the events of that night, eventually entering Folsom State Prison and becoming a gang leader.

Fig. 20: Montoya Santana reclaiming his masculinity after killing his rapist in *American Me*.

The male rape scene in *American Me* is typical in that it is quick and lacks significant detail. Similarly, with the notable exception of *Deliverance* (1972), male rape is hardly ever depicted outside of a prison. This stands in stark contrast to movies in which female characters are raped, from Sam Peckinpah's *Straw Dogs* (1971) to Gasper Noe's *Irreversible* (2003), where the scenes can take place anywhere and be agonisingly long. The women-in-prison exploitation subgenre frequently fetishises rape, but one movie stands out for its more complicated portrayal: Michael Miller's *Jackson County Jail* (1976). The rape of Dinah Hunter (Yvette Mimieux) by an officer is particularly difficult to watch, emphasising violation as violence above all else. The lack of any titillating details as well as the inclusion of the rapist's self-loathing and longing for forgiveness in the aftermath reveal the genuine horrors of the event. The scene's brutality makes it hard to feel anything but satisfaction when a traumatised Dinah beats the jailer to death with the stool from her cell. Jayne Loader argues that the scene does little 'for the women who continue to be brutalized and raped inside jails and out of them' because the film offers 'individual solutions to complex social problems: kill criminals rather than abolish the causes of crime' (1985: 338). Still, *Jackson County Jail*'s realism induces genuine revulsion and sets it apart from other films of its type.

Not all sexual encounters in prison films involve rape, but Hollywood's love of violence and fear of two men having sex is clearly evident in Alan Parker's *Midnight Express* (1978). Based on the bestselling autobiography by Billy Hayes and William Hoffer, with a script by a young Oliver Stone, the film tells the story of Hayes' sentence in a Turkish prison for drug possession and his harrowing escape. Hayes reveals in the book that in reality he fell in love with another man and had an intimate affair in prison. In the film, however, that relationship is transformed into a friendship with a fictional character named Erich (Norbert Weisser). A homoeroticism is suggested between the men by having them bathe and do yoga together, but when the two men share a kiss in the shower, Hayes gently turns Erich down by kissing his hand and walking away. Erich then disappears from the film entirely, being released soon after. The film deserves some progressive credit for showing a moment of intimacy between two men, but the scene is so dark and filled with so much steam that viewers can barely see anything.

Instead of showing two men engaged in a loving sexual relationship, the film renders it virtually invisible. It also recasts sexual imagery as violence in two key scenes and openly presents it in graphic detail. During a voice-over in which Hayes explains the rules of the prison to his girlfriend, he states: 'You can stab or shoot somebody below the waste, but not above because that's intent to kill. So everybody runs around stabbing everyone else in the ass.' As Hayes speaks, the film shows a man approaching another prisoner with a knife and stabbing him until the man falls to the ground bleeding. In one of the film's most infamous scenes, Hayes has a mental breakdown and violently attacks the prison snitch, Rifki (Paolo Bonacelli), by biting the man's tongue off and spitting it out in slow motion. These two incidents of anal and oral penetration – 'stabbing' a man 'in the ass' and putting a tongue in another man's mouth – are the film's way of displacing uncomfortable sex with acceptable violence. By doing so, the character of Billy Hayes doesn't alienate a heteronormative audience that so closely identifies with him throughout the film.

Incidents of rape are suggested throughout *Midnight Express*, but rape becomes explicit and central to Hayes' escape toward the end. When Hayes' attempt to bribe a prison guard backfires, he is dragged into a room by the sadistic guard, Hamidou (Paul Smith). When Hamidou attempts to rape Hayes, he pushes the guard against the wall, impaling his head on a hook. The death of Hamidou allows Hayes to take his uniform and slip out the door unnoticed. Farmer points out that by the end of the film, 'Hayes is a broken man; physically exhausted and barely able to communicate, and his sanity is questionable. Given Hayes' deteriorated physical and mental condition, his forceful resistance suggests that he can withstand anything except rape' (2008: 110).

In more recent films, the threat of rape does more than help certain characters escape. Daniel LaChance argues convincingly that prison movies like *The Shawshank Redemption* (1994) and *American History X* (1998) show white characters actually benefitting from being the victims of rape. While noting that depicting rape as curative of other ills is 'obviously repellent' (2015: 175), he states:

> The prison is not a painful, potentially guilt-inducing symptom of a white establishment's obsession with control, but a valuable therapeutic experience that teaches white men to let go of their destructive obsession with agency in their personal lives. Even the horror of rape within the prison walls becomes perversely reconfigured as a therapeutic mechanism for learning to let go, for experiencing a rewarding release from the sense of alienation and atomization that prompts their efforts to exert or maintain control over the world. In the end, the legal and extra-legal violence of punishment is troublingly justified in these texts as a necessary part of a process of personal rehabilitation. (2015: 163)

In Tony Kaye's *American History X*, Derek Vinyard (Edward Norton) is a neo-Nazi who is sentenced to three years in prison for killing two black men trying to steal his truck. Derek's racism is fueled by his father's teachings and his death at the hands of two black drug dealers while he was on call as a fire fighter. While in prison Derek joins with members of the Aryan Brotherhood but becomes disillusioned with them for their interactions with other gang members and drug dealing. When he finally breaks with the Aryans, Derek is raped in the shower by members of the Brotherhood for his betrayal. After the rape, Derek begins listening to the advice of his former teacher and starts becoming friendly with a black inmate named Lamont (Guy Torry) with whom he works in the prison laundry. LaChance notes: 'The film suggests that the degrading experience of being violently leveled down ultimately softens Derek and opens his mind to voices of reason that had, before his rape, been unable to influence him' (2015: 173). By the time Derek leaves prison, he is a changed man who renounces his past and attempts to prevent his younger brother from going down the same path he did.

Of *The Shawshank Redemption*, LaChance argues that 'the violent paces through which the white male protagonist is put are designed not to test and affirm his whiteness and manhood, but to expose and address a numbness, a detachment or emptiness that is an undesirable byproduct of being a white-collar white man' (2015: 177). When Andy Dufresne (Tim Robbins) enters prison he possesses a stoic detachment, a quality he also exhibited during his murder trial, which helped lead to his conviction. At one point, Andy says to Red (Morgan Freeman): 'My wife used to say I'm a hard man to know. Like a closed book. Complained about it all the time. She was beautiful. I loved her. But I guess I couldn't show it enough. I killed her, Red. I didn't pull the trigger. But I drove her away. That's why she died. Because of me, the way I am.' LaChance argues that the rapes Andy endures help him recognise his own 'masculine hardness', and 'Just as Derek begins to soften when he strikes up a friendship with Lamont in *American History X*, Andy's coldness subsides over the course of the film as his friendship with Red grows' (2015: 181). The exact reasons for this 'therapeutic' depiction of rape are difficult to ascertain. LaChance attributes it to 'white anxiety, one focused not on a menacing racial other, but on white masculinity itself' (2015: 162).

What is certain is that attitudes toward incarceration began to change in the 1990s, becoming more punitive and pervasive. The final section of this chapter examines two key prison films from the 1990s by the same director, Frank Darabont: the one discussed above, *The Shawshank Redemption*, and *The Green Mile*. Both address race and identity, but they do it through a nostalgic lens that draws on punitive eras of the past while speaking to a 1990s present that witnessed one of the largest growths in the prison population to date.

### Prison movies in the 1990s

In 1994, President Clinton signed into law the Violent Crime Control and Law Enforcement Act, the largest crime bill in US history. At a time when crime was actually going down, the bill increased funds for additional law enforcement officials and the construction of new prisons. In addition to creating the 'three strikes' law, which instituted mandatory life sentences for repeat offenders, the bill expanded the number of offences which were eligible for the death penalty. It also increased the problem of mass incarceration, which disproportionately affected the lives of millions of African Americans. In response, many prison films were released during the decade, but one year in particular, 1999, has the distinction of producing five major films in which black men were convicted for crimes they didn't commit: *The Hurricane*, *Life*, *True Crime*, *The Green Mile* and the TV movie *A Lesson Before Dying*. Clearly, by decade's end, matters of racial injustice were coming into view, but on the whole, the array of prison movies produced within the 1990s suggest an undeniable looking away from the very real problems of the criminal justice system. Crowd-pleasing big budget action films, such as *The Rock* (1995), *Face/Off* (1997) and *Con Air* (1997), used prisons as settings for thrills rather than sites of serious societal contemplation. Even Ted Demme's *Life*, starring Eddie Murphy and Martin Lawrence, focuses far more on the relationship of its stars than on the outrageous injustice of their decades-long imprisonment.

In her famous essay 'Unspeakable Things Unspoken', Toni Morrison ponders the absence of African-Americans in so much of American literature:

> We can agree, I think, that invisible things are not necessarily 'not-there'; that a void may be empty, but is not a vacuum. In addition, certain absences are so stressed, so ornate, so planned, they call attention to themselves... Looking at the scope of American literature, I can't help thinking that the question should never have been 'Why am I, an Afro-American, absent from it?' It is not a particularly interesting query anyway. The spectacularly interesting question is 'What intellectual feats had to be performed by the author or his critic to erase me from a society seething with my presence, and what effect has that performance had on the work?' What are the strategies of escape from knowledge? Of willful oblivion? (1989: 11–12)

The questions Morrison asks are useful in thinking about the strange 'intellectual feats' two of the decade's most popular prison films, *The*

*Shawshank Redemption* and *The Green Mile*, perform in order to avoid looking at racism and injustice directly. At a time when one might expect gritty realism, these two films embrace nostalgia and the supernatural, qualities that were rarely employed in prison films prior. Instead of verity, one film presents a fabled white hero who is wrongly (it is implied) convicted of killing his wife, and the other depicts a magical, innocent black man who gladly solves the problems of his troubled white jailers.

Adapted from stories by Stephen King, both *The Shawshank Redemption* and *The Green Mile* were written and directed by Frank Darabont. As such, they contain many of the same themes and preoccupations. As a genre, prison movies beget very few sequels (no one really wants to see *The Shawshank Redemption II: Back to Shawshank*). Still, with the common prison settings and the pairings of white and black protagonists, it's hard not to see the story of Paul Edgecomb (Tom Hanks) and John Coffey (Michael Clarke Duncan) as a continuation of Andy Dusfresne and Red's. Much has been written about Hollywood's love of 'the magical black man', a mysterious character invested with extraordinary power who appears from nowhere to improve the life of a white character rather than his own. This is certainly the case in *The Green Mile*, as John Coffey cures Paul's bladder infection and sex life, as well as the warden's wife's brain tumor, only to be electrocuted for the privilege. Around the same time as *The Green Mile*, other magical black characters appeared in *What Dreams May Come* (1998), *The Family Man* (2000), *The Legend of Bagger Vance* (2000) and *Unbreakable* (2000). Some critics have attributed the phenomenon to white screenwriters' lack of knowledge of African-American culture. Others, such as Heather J. Hicks, attribute it to a 'crisis surrounding white masculinity' (2003: 28). Linda Williams calls attention to 'the remarkable extent to which the establishment of white virtue rests upon a paradoxical administration of pain and death to the black body so that white people may weep' (2001: 20). Regardless the exact reason, there's little doubt that characters like John Coffey are a product of white wish fulfillment. Although Red in *The Shawshank Redemption* doesn't fit all of the criteria, he too guides a white character through troubled times while maintaining a mystery about him. We know little of his past, and like Coffey, he has no history. As a character says of Coffey, it's 'like he dropped out of the sky'.

Coffey and Red serve several functions to Paul and Andy. At the end of *The Shawshank Redemption*, Red joins Andy on a beautiful Pacific beach

Fig. 21: Red's reunion with Andy on the beaches of Mexico in *The Shawshank Redemption*.

where Red will presumably help Andy run his burgeoning hotel and fishing business. In the letter Andy leaves for Red in the field, he tells him 'hope is a good thing' and 'no good thing ever dies'. As his words and life attest, Andy's entire mentality is forward-looking. Red, however, is backward-looking. As the film's narrator, Red, from somewhere in the present of Mexico, reflects not on his own difficult life, but on the life of his extraordinary friend. In telling all of the incredible things that Andy endured and accomplished, Red succeeds in making Andy the stuff of legend. In similar fashion, Paul in *The Green Mile* looks back on his time as a prison guard and his encounter with the miraculous John Coffey. It's only at the very end of the film that viewers learn that Coffey possessed the 108-year-old Paul with some form of eternal life. Both films then, in essence, depict a black man immortalising a white man. It could be argued that Paul's story immortalises John Coffey, but as Paul tells his listener in the nursing home: 'I haven't spoken of these things for a long time, Ellie, over sixty years.' At the end, as Paul explains to Ellie that he has lived to see everyone he ever loved die, the film is careful to show Ellie, his sole listener, in her coffin, suggesting John's story will not be passed down. Similarly, although Red is a great storyteller, he will likely be forgotten. There is nothing that suggests Red is writing a memoir. Rather, Red makes Andy the subject of an oral tale, one that will be amended and kept alive by others throughout the ages. Before leaving the halfway house where Brooks carved 'Brooks was here' in the wood before committing suicide, Red carves 'So was Red', signifying the scrawl will be the only evidence of his existence.

*The Shawshank Redemption*'s assertion then that 'no good thing ever dies' implies a kind of positive, eternal value to the things that Paul and Andy represent: hard work, perseverance, rationality and decency. But if Coffey and Red do not endure, what then are they? For one thing, they are criminals. Although both characters are endearing, they do not possess the same 'goodness' as Paul and Andy. When Andy asks Red if he's innocent of murder, Red acknowledges he's the 'only guilty man in Shawshank'. Similarly, although Coffey is innocent of the crimes he's convicted of and maintains a child-like quality throughout the film, he enacts a vengeful, Old Testament-style justice on 'Wild Bill' Wharton by compelling Percy to murder him in cold blood. He further exhibits no mercy when he infects Percy with the sickness he drew out of the warden's wife, rendering him insane and confined to a mental institution. Even though Paul's job is to execute prisoners, the film's setting in the Great Depression makes it understandable. As Heather J. Hicks points out, 'the film implicitly provides a rationale for the men's choice of work. That is, its recurrent visual and verbal allusions to the scarcity of jobs provide an excuse for the guards' enthusiastic relationship to such seemingly morally questionable and dispiriting work' (2003: 37–38). Paul performs his unpleasant job with the utmost respect for the prisoners and the process. When one of the trustees makes a joke during an execution run-through and the guards start laughing, Paul is quick to scold: 'We'll be doing this for real tomorrow night. I don't want anybody remembering some stupid joke like that and gettin' goin' again.' After Coffey's execution, he requests a transfer to a boy's correctional facility where he can prevent kids from heading down the wrong path in life. Paul's shift from necessary work to good work validates him as good man who has lived a serviceable life.

In *The Shawshank Redemption*, Andy too is involved in a nefarious system, laundering money for Warden Norton, but he has little choice. When he attempts to quit, Norton tells him: 'Nothing stops. Nothing. Or you will do the hardest time there is. No more protection from the guards. I'll pull you out of that one-bunk Hilton and cast you down with the sodomites.' As Andy says to Red: 'You know the funny thing is, on the outside, I was an honest man, straight as an arrow. I had to come to prison to be a crook.' Red, however, came in a killer. Andy, by contrast, learns the system and ultimately exhibits a virtue that redeems himself and Shawshank when he reveals the corruption to the media. As Peter Gutierrez points out, 'the state is prepared to avert its eyes until a whistle-blower not only steps up, but secures his own safety' (2013: 102). Red, on the other hand, is simply released, having accomplished not much more than serving his time. His greater, redemptive cause is the valorisation of Andy Dusfresne.

The most obvious thing both movies have in common is their set-tings in the past. *The Green Mile* takes place in 1935, and *The Shawshank Redemption* begins its story in 1947 and moves forward to the 1960s. Neither film, however, is interested in foregrounding issues of race. White and black prisoners get along just fine in Shawshank. In *The Green Mile*, it's really only Percy who spouts racial epithets at John Coffey, but that racism is undermined by the fact that he's also a sadistic misanthrope and equal opportunity hater. In a decade that saw the beating of Rodney King, the 1992 Los Angeles Riots, the racial divide of the O. J. Simpson trial, the moral panic surrounding Ice-T's song 'Cop Killer', and President Bill Clinton's coining of the term 'super-predator' to describe immoral black youth, *The Shawshank Redemption* and *The Green Mile* seem like wistful throwbacks to better times that never were. As Hicks points out, 'On the most fundamental level, *The Green Mile* can be seen as a nos-talgic celebration of an era when white men made the rules' (2003: 42). Charles I. Nero observes of *The Shawshank Redemption* that Andy and Red are confined to a place 'outside history' where racism and the civil rights movement never happened. He further notes: 'Once outside of prison, they are excused from the aftermath of the movement by being relocated to a so-called place "with no memory"' (2004: 68). In *The Shawshank Redemption*, Andy confesses to Red that he created a fictional character named Randall Stephens, 'a phantom, an apparition', in order to cover up the real corruption of Shawshank. If viewers look to *The Shawshank Redemption* and *The Green Mile* to uncover accurate representations of race relations in the 1990s, they are, in many ways, going to do exactly what the white, upper-middle-class Andy planned: 'they're going to wind up chasing a figment of my imagination.'

The looking away of the 1990s became harder and harder to maintain as the damaging consequences of mass incarceration became increasingly undeniable in the 2000s. Such visibility, coupled with cultural shifts in attitudes toward torture, 'enemy combatants' and 'detainees' in a post-9/11 world changed prison movies yet again, topics explored in the following chapter.

## AFTERWORD: POST-9/11 PRISON MOVIES AND THE ERA OF MASS INCARCERATION

'The techniques change, the victims change, but it's still a question. How do these things happen? How are they institutionalized?'
*The Experimenter* (2015)

In a 2015 article for *The Atlantic* entitled 'The Black Family in the Age of Mass Incarceration', Ta-Nehisi Coates laid out some sobering statistics:

In absolute terms, America's prison and jail population from 1970 until today has increased sevenfold, from some 300,000 people to 2.2 million. The United States now accounts for less than 5 per cent of the world's inhabitants – and about 25 per cent of its incarcerated inhabitants. In 2000, one in 10 black males between the ages of 20 and 40 was incarcerated – 10 times the rate of their white peers. In 2010, a third of all black male high-school dropouts between the ages of 20 and 39 were imprisoned, compared with only 13 percent of their white peers.

Such deplorable numbers raise troubling questions about the state of civil rights, race relations and law enforcement in the twenty-first century. In addition, in the years following the 9/11 attacks on the World Trade Center, human rights groups have been increasingly concerned with the rights of detainees, inmate privacy, unfair trials, racial profiling, secret detention, illegal extradition and prisoner abuse. Non-profit organisations such as the Innocence Project have used DNA technology to exonerate hundreds of wrongly-convicted citizens, many of whom were serving time on death row. Other organisations have called attention to the highly questionable morality of capital punishment, as well as the efficacy of lethal injection in providing a merciful death. Not surprisingly, both fiction and documentary filmmakers have made such issues the subjects of their films. Documentary's capacity 'to open our eyes to worlds available to us but, for one reason or another, not perceived' (Barnouw 1993: 3) has been utilised by directors for years to shed light on the darker aspects of prison life.

One of the best examples is Cinda Firestone's *Attica* (1974), which uses innovative editing techniques to examine the four-day-long 1971 inmate uprising that left 43 people dead. As Linda Ruth Williams and Michael Hammond observe, *Attica* suggests 'knowledge is grounded in contestation and contradiction. Encouraged to come to his or her own conclusions, the viewer is in a position to honour the prisoners' revolutionary and fatal demands: that is, not only to better understand the tragedy, but to testify as well to the violent power of misrepresentation in the mainstream media on vulnerable minorities' (2006: 207). More recently, well-known directors such as Alex Gibney in *Taxi to the Dark Side* (2007) and Errol Morris in *Standard Operating Procedure* (2008) have used non-traditional documentary techniques to challenge official versions of events and uncover nuanced layers of truths. Amateur filmmakers and non-profit organisations are also playing an important role in exposing the inequities of the criminal justice system. In contrast to the exploitative prison reality shows mentioned in the introduction, some television documentaries and *cinéma vérité*-style videos have given voice to people not often 'available to us' and 'not perceived'. This chapter doesn't attempt to analyse these films so much as call attention to them. Many such films not only speak for themselves, they speak for those who can't.

*Mass incarceration*

In the same way that Eugene Jarecki's *Why We Fight* (2005) examined the military-industrial complex that arose after World War II, his film *The House*

*I Live In* (2012) scrutinises the prison-industrial complex that began mate-
rialising alongside 'the war on drugs' in the 1970s. It uses archival footage,
talking heads and interviews to show the effects of both drug and institutional abuse. Jarecki begins by quietly asserting himself into the narrative,
relating his personal connection to an African-American woman named
Nannie Jeter who helped raise him in his white middle-class neighbor-
hood. Jarecki tells us: 'Our families were close. And her children and grand-
children were my playmates growing up. But as we got older, I saw many
of them struggling, with poverty, joblessness, crime, and worse.' When he
asks Nannie what she thinks went wrong, her answer is simple: drugs. As
David Simon, creator of *The Wire*, states in the film, 'what drugs haven't
destroyed, the war against them has'. The film reveals how anti-drug laws
have always been about race in the US. In the 1800s, drugs like cocaine
and opium were legal and used primarily by middle-class whites. When the
Chinese began taking jobs away from white Americans in the latter part of
the nineteenth century, lawmakers made opium illegal in California. In the
1930s, marijuana became demonised to target Mexican workers. Because
politicians couldn't make a race illegal, they made habits illegal. Civil
rights advocate Michelle Alexander states in the film: 'You know in any war

Fig. 22: A young man awaits a mandatory minimum sentence in *The House I Live In*.

you've got to have an enemy. And when you think about the impact particularly on poor people of colour, there are more African-Americans under correctional control today in prison or jail on probation or parole than were enslaved in 1850, a decade before the Civil War began. And that's something we haven't been willing to look in the mirror and ask ourselves, what's really going on?'

One of the things that's going on is the profitability of the prison system. In a startling scene, *The House I Live In* enters a trade convention, attended by almost exclusively white patrons, where companies promote their latest restraint chairs, tasers and high-dollar copies of the Koran to be distributed to desiring inmates. The film shows how corporations and for-profit prisons have a vested interest in maintaining the war on drugs. The film also gives voice to judges and corrections officers frustrated by mandatory minimum sentences and the lack of rehabilitation programmes that might prevent the revolving door of recidivism.

The effects of incarceration, of course, are not just felt by prisoners. One particular advocacy initiative entitled Echoes of Incarceration, which is funded by multiple non-profit organisations, allows the children of incarcerated parents to make documentaries chronicling their own experiences. Their stated goal on their website is 'to give voice to one of the largest and most invisible social issues of our times, and to harness the intelligence, energy, and creativity of young people to rethink our understandings of crime and punishment'. Another film produced by an advocacy group is Mathew Pillischer's *Broken on All Sides: Race, Mass Incarceration, and New Visions for Criminal Justice in the U.S.* (2012). The film is the centrepiece of a grassroots tour to prompt discussions and educate people on how to dismantle the prison-industrial complex.

Though an older documentary, and not one that deals with mass incarceration *per se*, *The Farm: Angola U.S.A.* (1998) is a still-relevant and fascinating look at the largest maximum-security prison in the nation, housing over 5,000 inmates, 77 per cent of whom are black, and 85 per cent of whom will die inside its walls. A former slave plantation, Angola is a multi-million dollar working farm that pays inmates just 4 cents an hour, a disturbing condition highlighted by opening images of men singing and working the farm, looking as if they could be from the eighteenth century. The film follows the lives of six inmates and begins with the induction of George Crawford, a 22-year-old African-American man convicted of murder and given a life sentence without the possibility of parole. As the bus takes Crawford into the prison, the voice-over states: 'Louisiana is known to have the harshest sentencing in the country. And while the common perception is that prisoners don't serve their full terms, for those heading to Angola Prison, life means life.' As Crawford waits in line to enter the prison for the first time, a white guard turns to the camera and says: 'We're all guaranteed a job, we have good job security'. During an orientation meeting, one of the old-timers tells newcomers: 'One of the things you find out while in penitentiary is that everybody who's close to you over a period of time, they're all going to fade away.' He then tells the prisoners not to give up hope, advice that falls on blank faces. Among the other prisoners profiled is a man who is clearly reformed but has no chance of getting out, and an elderly inmate who chooses to be buried inside the prison rather than in the family plot, something his relatives find cruel and struggle to understand. Nominated for an Academy Award for Best Documentary, *The Farm: Angola U.S.A.* is a difficult film to watch at times, but it leaves an indelible impression about the legacy of slavery, the chain gang, and the prison farm system. In 2009, the same filmmakers made *The Farm: 10 Down*, which follows up with the same surviving inmates.

## Capital punishment

Perhaps the best known Hollywood film about capital punishment is Tim Robbins' *Dead Man Walking* (1995), based on the memoir by Sister Helen Prejean, a Louisiana nun. In the film, Prejean (Susan Sarandon) becomes the spiritual advisor to Matthew Poncelet (Sean Penn), a prisoner on death row convicted of the murders of two teenagers. Wisely, *Dead Man Walking* never tries to make Poncelet a particularly sympathetic character. Instead, its emotional force rests in how its heroine doggedly pursues a stay of execution out of principle rather than personal attachment.

It's a narrative approach to capital punishment also used by a radically different filmmaker in a very different film, Werner Herzog's documentary *Into the Abyss* (2011). In the film, Herzog travels to Huntsville, Texas, to interview Michael Perry and Jason Burkett, two men convicted of murder. As Herzog speaks with Perry just eight days before his scheduled execution date, he tells him: 'I have the feeling that destiny, in a way, has dealt you a very bad deck of cards. It does not exonerate you. And when I talk to you, it does not necessarily mean that I have to like you. But I respect you. And you're a human being and I think human beings should not be executed, simple as that.' Herzog delves into the murders the men committed, underscoring the callousness and brutality of their crimes. Rather than exploring the sociological reasons why the boys did what they did, Herzog makes the point that no matter what the causes, personal or societal failures, no one has the right to kill them. In a section subtitled 'The Protocol of Death', Herzog talks to Fred Allen, a former guard of Huntsville's death row who oversaw over 120 executions, sometimes two per week. He first reveals how he took pride in doing his job with the utmost professionalism. He then tells the story of how after putting a woman to death, he began to shake uncontrollably and see visions of the dead in their cells. Unable to do the job anymore, he quit, giving up his pension. His conclusion, as he tells Herzog, is that 'nobody has the right to take another life. I don't care if it's the law.'

Adrian Shergold's *Pierrepoint: The Last Hangman* (2005) makes a somewhat similar point. A drama about the UK's most prolific executioner, who did his job for over twenty years, *Pierrepoint* examines the emotional toll such a career takes on a man. Shergold shows Albert Pierrepoint (Timothy Spall) to be a man who approaches his job with detachment and the utmost professionalism, carefully measuring rope and calculating the height and weight of his 'clients' so as to do the most efficient job possible. Pierrepoint is so good at his job that he is personally requested by Field Marshall Montgomery to hang over two hundred convicted Nazis. The assembly line nature of those executions, however, begin to weaken his resolve and awaken his conscience. When his identity as a hangman is made public, he is at first celebrated for executing so many Nazis, but as the UK's attitude toward the death penalty began to shift in the 1950s, so did its feelings toward Pierrepoint. The film is clearly anti-capital punishment, but it never demonises the man. It simply shows him as a meticulous worker who, like Fred Allen, eventually couldn't take it anymore.

Although it's difficult to identify with a man like Albert Pierrepoint, it's simply impossible to like the man profiled in Errol Morris's documentary *Mr. Death: The Rise and Fall of Fred A. Leuchter* (1999). Leuchter, a chain smoking, coffee-addicted engineer of sorts spent the bulk of his career advising prisons on the proper uses of electric chairs, gas chambers, gallows and lethal injections. Though proclaiming to be disturbed by the suffering inefficient death devices can cause, Leuchter never once questions the morality of what he's doing. His lack of a moral compass eventually leads him to become involved with a group of Holocaust deniers who bring him to Auschwitz to 'prove' the gas chambers never existed. Hailed as a hero by one group and a fool by everyone else, Leuchter comes across as a man fueled more by hubris than hate, but whose mentality is nevertheless dangerous.

An excellent television documentary that explores the death penalty in multiple ways is *Life and Death Row* (2014), a three-part series from the BBC whose episodes are entitled 'Punishment', 'Judgement' and 'Crisis Stage'. The series covers a young man on death row for the murders of his girlfriend's parents, a 22-year-old man who killed eight family members, and a young law student fighting to keep a client from facing capital punishment.

Lastly, Steve James and Peter Gilbert's documentary *At the Death House Door* (2008) follows something of a familiar pattern for films profiling people intimately involved in the death penalty procedure. From 1982 to 1995, prison chaplain Carroll Pickett witnessed the executions of 95 inmates at the Texas State Penitentiary at Huntsville, the same prison Werner Herzog visited in *Into the Abyss*. Once a strong advocate for the death penalty, Pickett's views changed when he saw the execution of Carlos De Luna, a man who was most certainly innocent of the charge of murder. The film reviews evidence that exonerates De Luna, but its real focus is the evolution of a man's views. Pickett is revealed to be a compassionate man who used to spend the entire day with inmates on the day they were to be convicted. Toward the end of the film, Pickett says: 'Now they bring him in at 4 pm and two hours later, it's time to kill him.' The film's director, Steve James, made one of the best documentaries of the 1990s with *Hoop Dreams* (1994). *At the Death House Door* is arguably one of the best documentaries of the following decade, and it's certainly one of the most profound documentaries on capital punishment to date.

*Torture*

Perhaps it's merely a coincidence that 2015 saw the release of *The Experimenter* and *The Stanford Prison Experiment*, films that reminded viewers of Stanley Milgram's 1961 electric shock experiment that revealed people's obedience to authority and Philip Zimbardo's 1971 prison guard experiment that revealed the cognitive dissonance of abuse. Or perhaps enough time has passed to seriously reflect on the consequences of changes in US policy toward detainees and enemy combatants implemented during the Bush/Cheney/Rumsfeld years. Regardless, prisoner abuse at Abu Ghraib and Guantanamo Bay has been the subject of several recent films.

As early as 2005, PBS's *Frontline* shed light on the internal debates about 'coercive interrogation' in the Bush Administration in an episode called 'The Torture Question'. Errol Morris's *Standard Operating Procedure*, however, was the first feature-length documentary to examine the atrocities that took place at Abu Ghraib during the Iraq War. Morris organises the documentary according to the damning photographs of prisoner abuse that were taken by the guards themselves. As a relentless pursuer of the truth in films like *The Thin Blue Line* (1988) and *The Fog of War* (2003), Morris investigates the deeper stories surrounding each of the photos, not accepting what they portray at face value. In a sense, he interrogates the images themselves by having the people involved with them provide context and additional information that fall outside the frames. At one point, one of the men charged with determining what to charge the soldiers with states: 'When you look at this whole case as one great big media event, you kind of lose focus. These pictures actually depict several separate incidents of possible abuse or possible standard operating procedure. All you can do is present what you know is to be factual. You can't bring emotion or politics into the court.' As he speaks, Morris shows a series of photographs, all of which look like they depict abuse. As the film unfolds, it becomes increasingly clear that there really is no difference between 'abuse' and 'standard operating procedure', other than the consequences the determinations have on the soldiers in the photos.

Morris presents soldier after soldier expressing their initial shock at seeing the treatment of prisoners, revealing they knew that what was happening was both illegal and immoral. Eventually, however, each one explains how they fell in line and either kept quiet or participated in the abuse because authorities told them to do so. In a particularly telling moment, one soldier describes seeing a buddy of his named Freddy suddenly draw an 'X' on a prisoner's chest and punch him as hard as he could. The soldier says to the camera: 'I'm like, what? Who are you and what did you do with Freddy?' At times, the soldiers seem genuinely baffled by what occurred and seem to lack a certain amount of genuine introspection. What the majority of them are clear about, however, is expressed by one soldier: 'Somebody caught our administration with their pants down. That's it. They're pissed off at that. You can kill people off camera. You can shoot people. You can, you know, blow their heads off. As long as it's not on camera, you're okay. But if it's on camera, you're done.' Although it's clear the soldiers are scapegoats for higher authorities, their true lack of ownership of what they did is what makes the documentary particularly disturbing.

The 2007 documentary *Ghosts of Abu Ghraib*, directed by Rory Kennedy, takes a more sympathetic look at the soldiers. It focuses far more on the administration's culpability in setting a tone that the soldiers were either encouraged or ordered to follow. It explains the history of the Geneva Convention and traces the administration's decision to release the US from the binding international agreement in 2002. The logic was, since Al Qaeda didn't adhere to the Geneva Conventions, the US didn't have to either. The film also chronicles how the administration began to define torture so narrowly that virtually anything was allowed. Unlike *Standard Operating Procedure*, *Ghosts of Abu Ghraib* includes interviews with prisoners who were held at the prison. Even as prisoners describe the abuse they endured, viewers are compelled to blame generals, the CIA and bureaucrats for the actions of the soldiers. As one commentator says: 'Abu Ghraib is a great example of bureaucratic virtuosity in handling a scandal.' The film does not let the soldiers off the hook, but even the soldier who received the most media attention for being a sadist, Charles Graner, takes on a more human dimension in the film. Taken together, *Standard Operating Procedure* and *Ghosts of Abu Ghraib* reveal both personal and systematic failure.

A fictionalised account of incidents at the prison appear in Luke Moran's *Boys of Abu Ghraib* (2014). Although the documentaries are far more effective in helping viewers understand what happened, Moran's film is notable for the way in which it depicts the soldiers as prisoners too. The soldiers sleep in cells, follow a dull routine day after day, have their stays extended and their leaves denied. At one point, the main character, Jack Farmer (Luke Moran), says: 'We do not fight terrorists; we fight boredom.' That boredom helps create the vacuum in which abuse thrives.

The other thing the film is notable for is in telling a prison story from the perspective of a guard. In this regard, the film shares a lot in common with Peter Sattler's *Camp X-Ray* (2014), a dramatised version of life at the Guantánamo Bay prison. Both films show their protagonists developing friendships with one of the inmates and questioning the morality of what they and the military are doing to them. *Camp X-Ray* is the more thoughtful of the two films, as PFC Amy Cole (Kristen Stewart) begins to empathise with a difficult prisoner named Ali who reaches his breaking point and tries to commit suicide. Like *Boys of Abu Ghraib*, *Camp X-Ray* shows soldiers humiliating and dehumanising the prisoners. By the end of the film, Cole finishes up her tour at Guantánamo having come to a new understanding about the enemy and her own government. Ali, however, remains in his cell, with no hope of release in sight.

Michael Winterbottom's *The Road to Guantánamo* (2006) is about the 'Tipton Three', British citizens who were captured in Afghanistan and detained at Guantánamo for over two years. Winterbottom produces an interesting mixture of dramatisation and documentary to unfold the Kafkaesque nightmare the three men endured before being released. Held in a place beyond the law, without formal charges and access to lawyers, the three men spend their days in wire cells and undergo exhausting inter-rogations. There's little by way of plot, but that's also the case with life at Guantánamo itself. The inclusion of testimonials by the actual Tipton Three provide insights into the events that go on there. Because of Guantánamo's intense secrecy, informed documentaries are few, with the exception of the short film, *Guantánamo: Blacked Out Bay* (2013).

Lastly, Alex Gibney's *Taxi to the Dark Side* is a documentary that serves as an indictment of the Bush administration's interrogation practices during the Afghan War. The film takes its title from a terrifying quote Dick Cheney offered during an appearance on *Meet the Press* shortly after 9/11: 'We also have to work through, sort of, the dark side, if you will. We've got to spend time in the shadows in the intelligence world. A lot of what needs to be done here will have to be done quietly, without any discussion, using sources and methods that are available to our intelligence agencies, if we're going to be successful.' The film begins by telling the story of an Afghan taxi driver named Dilawar who is falsely accused of being a terror-ist. He is arrested and taken to an American prison in Bagram, Afghanistan where he is brutally beaten and eventually killed during an interrogation session. No one was ever tried for murder or held responsible for Dilawar's death.

*Recidivism*

In *A Plague of Prisons*, Ernest Drucker points out that in the US over 700,000 prisoners are released each year; however, incarceration can have life-long effects:

> The adverse effects of incarceration on individual prisoners in-
> clude the ongoing consequences of poor health care services in
> prisons; failure of prison security to provide a safe environment
> (the ensuing rape, violence, and gang activity that have become
> a routine part of prison life); serious and persistent mental health
> problems and inadequate mental health care in prisons; and a
> paucity of addiction treatment and the absence of effective drug
> rehabilitation. [Thus] most do not stay outside very long: recidi-
> vism is massive, with about one-third of released prisoners rear-
> rested within the first twelve months, and two-thirds of released
> prisoners returning within three years. (2011: 214–15)

It is ironic that so many fictional prison movies focus on escape plans when in reality inmates need far more help fashioning survival plans once released.

The problem of recidivism, of course, is not limited to the US. One of the most compelling prison movies dealing with the vicious cycle of incarcera-tion is the British drama *Starred Up* (2013), directed by David Mackenzie and written by Jonathan Asser, an actual counselor who spent years work-ing in the largest prison in the United Kingdom, HP Prison Wandsworth. The film tells the story of Eric Love (Jack O'Connell), a 19-year-old inmate so violent he's been 'starred up' to an adult prison two years earlier than normal. Unlike prison films that show terrified inductees, *Starred Up* reveals Eric to be a seasoned veteran of prison life. Once in his cell, he immediately fashions a weapon out of a shaving razor and toothbrush and hides it in a light fixture. Shortly thereafter, he severely beats another inmate and battles a team of guards in riot gear before being placed in solitary. Because of Eric's young age, the prison counselor, Oliver Baumer

(Rupert Friend), convinces Deputy Governor Hayes (Sam Spruell) to let Eric join a therapy group specifically designed to help inmates deal with rage and anger. Eric, however, is housed in the same prison as his father, Neville (Ben Mendelsohn), who becomes jealous of Oliver's role as a thoughtful father figure to his son. During one of the group sessions, Neville bursts in and tells Oliver how to make Eric behave: 'Problem is you got to come down on him full throttle, else it won't register.' Eric hadn't seen his father, however, since he was five and feels anguish in his presence. Raised by the state after his mother died, Eric was sexually abused when he was ten and is serving time for attacking a man who harmed a woman his father calls a 'junky slut'. Throughout the film, Eric is pulled between his father's selfish brutishness and Oliver's judicious guidance.

Though Eric shows genuine improvement during his time in counseling, two parallel shots suggest his likely outcome. After Oliver is fired for protesting Eric's removal from the group, he departs though a revolving door. In the film's final scene, Eric says goodbye to his father who is being transferred to another prison after killing another inmate. As Eric walks back into the prison, the camera holds on a similar revolving door as it cycles around and around. Ultimately, *Starred Up* depicts a system more interested in warehousing inmates than in helping them rehabilitate, a mindset all-too-easily validated by statistics.

In *Are Prisons Obsolete?*, Angela Y. Davis make a provocative observation: 'How difficult it is to envision a social order that does not rely on the threat of sequestering people in dreadful places designed to separate

Fig. 23: The familiar image of the revolving door in *Starred Up*.

them from their communities and families. The prison is considered so "natural" that it is extremely hard to imagine life without it' (2003: 10). Even as prison movies have exposed the horrors of the 'dreadful places' they portray, they have no doubt affected the public imagination of prisons and contributed to the 'naturalisation' of the institution. If the image of a society without prisons is too utopian for most people to entertain, perhaps the prison genre may evolve to show genuine progressive strides and alternatives. As Ernest Drucker writes:

> While some societies still defend the most lurid responses to crimes ... most developed Western democracies show a long and clear trend away from those sorts of punishments. In developed nations (formerly including the United States) there has been a steady movement since World War II toward better prison conditions, shorter prison sentences, and more genuine and effective efforts at rehabilitation. (2011: 114)

Drucker's criticism of the United States remains valid, but there are indications of a cultural shift in thinking about incarceration. In January 2016, US President Barack Obama announced a series of prison reforms based on recommendations he received from the Justice Department. They included ending solitary confinement for juvenile offenders and expanding treatment options for the mentally ill. In addition, he has commuted more prison sentences than the previous seven presidents combined. Still, that number, 348, is a mere drop in the bucket for a carceral state of 2.2 million. The US Justice Department recently announced its plan to end its use of private, for-profit prisons, yet the move does not affect the use of private state prisons, which are far more numerous. President Obama has promised to close the prison at Guantánamo, and yet it remains open. And mass incarceration remains.

Prison movies call our attention to clandestine worlds, and that is in part their importance. At their best, they are calls for people to pay attention to suffering and be aware of how that suffering may affect themselves and others. Such a sentiment is best expressed by an ex-convict in the final line of the documentary *Attica*: 'Wake up, because nothing comes to a sleeper but a dream.'

# BIBLIOGRAPHY

Altman, Rick (1999) *Film/Genre*. London: British Film Institute.

Anon. (1955) 'Film Tells Familiar Tale: "Women's Prison" in Bow at Palace Theater', *New York Times*, February 3.

Baldwin, James (2011 [1976]) *The Devil Finds Work*. New York: Vintage.

Barnouw, Erik (1993) *Documentary: A History of the Non-fiction Film*. 2nd ed. New York: Oxford University Press.

Bloom, Barbara and David Steinhart (1993) *Why Punish the Children? A Reappraisal of the Children of Incarcerated Mothers in America*. San Francisco: National Council on Crime and Delinquency.

Blue, Ethan (2012) *Doing Time in the Depression: Everyday Life in Texas and California Prisons*. New York: New York University Press.

Book, Aaron S. (1999) 'Shame On You: An Analysis of Modern Shame Punishment as an Alternative to Incarceration', *William and Mary Law Review*, 40, 2, 653–86.

Bosworth, Mary (2010) *Explaining U.S. Imprisonment*. Los Angeles: Sage.

Bouchlin, Suzanne (2009) 'Women in Prison Movies as Feminist Juris-prudence', *Canadian Journal of Women and the Law*, 21, 19–34.

Buscombe, Edward (2012) 'The Idea of Genre in the American Cinema', in Barry Keith Grant (ed.) *Film Genre Reader IV*. Austin: University of Texas Press, 12–26.

Canby, Vincent (1979) 'Penitentiary: Jailhouse Blues', *New York Times*, 4 April.

_____ (1980) ''Alcatraz' Opens: With Clint Eastwood'. *New York Times*, 22 June.

Chare, Nicholas (2015) 'Fugitive Aesthetics: Embodiment, Sexuality and *Escape from Alcatraz*', *Paragraph*, 38, 1, 37–54.

Cheatwood, Derral (1998) 'Prison Movies: Films About Adult Male Civilian Prisoners: 1929–1995', in Frankie Y. Bailey and Donna C. Hale (eds) *Popular Culture, Crime and Justice*. Belmont, CA: Wadsworth.

Christianson, Scott (1998) *With Liberty for Some: 500 Years of Imprisonment in America*. Boston: Northeastern University Press.

Ciasullo, Ann (2008) 'Containing 'Deviant' Desire: Lesbianism, Hetero-sexuality, and the Women-in-Prison Narrative', *The Journal of Popular Culture*, 41, 2, 195–223.

Clover, Carol J. (2002) 'Her Body, Himself: Gender in the Slasher Film', in Mark Jancovich (ed.) *Horror: The Film Reader*. London: Routledge, 77–90.

Coates, Ta-Nehisi (2015) 'The Black Family in the Age of Mass Incarceration', *The Atlantic*, October, 60–84.

Cox, Stephen (2009) *The Big House: Image and Reality of the American Prison*. New Haven, CT: Yale University Press.

Crowther, Bruce (1989) *Captured on Film: The Prison Movie*. London: B. T. Batsford.

Davis, Angela Y. (2003) *Are Prisons Obsolete?* New York: Seven Stories Press.

Davis, David A. (2010) '*I Am a Fugitive from a Chain Gang!* and the Mat-eriality of Southern Depravity', *Mississippi Quarterly*, 63, 3/4, 399–417.

Death Penalty Information Center (2016) *History of the Death Penalty*; http://www.deathpenaltyinfo.org/part-i-history-death-penalty

Denning, Michael (1997) *The Cultural Front: The Laboring of American Culture in the Twentieth Century*. London: Verso.

Desser, David (2014) 'Science Fiction', in Lester Friedman, David Desser, Sarah Kozloff, Martha Nochimson and Stephen Prince (eds) in *An Introduction to Film Genres*. New York: W. W. Norton, 324–67.

Drucker, Ernest (2011) *A Plague of Prisons: The Epidemiology of Mass Incarceration in America*. New York: The New Press.

Dyer, Richard (1993) *The Matter of Images: Essays on Representations*. London: Routledge.

____ (1997) *White*. London: Routledge.

Elsaesser, Thomas (2012 [1986]) 'Tales of Sound and Fury: Observations on the Family Melodramas' in Barry Keith Grant (ed.) *Film Genre Reader IV*. Austin: University of Texas Press, 433–62.

Farmer, Angela (2008) 'The Worst Fate: Male Rape as Masculinity Epideixis in James Dickey's *Deliverance* and the American Prison Narrative', *Atenea*, 28, 1, 103–15.

Findley, Mary (2008) 'The Prisoner, the Pen, and the Number One Fan: *Misery* as a Prison Film', in Tony Magistrale (ed.) *The Films of Stephen King: From Carrie to Secret Window*. New York: Palgrave Macmillian, 91–100.

Fischer, Lucy (1996) *Film, Motherhood, Genre*. Princeton, NJ: Princeton University Press.

Foucault, Michel (1977) *Discipline and Punish: The Birth of the Prison*. New York: Vintage.

Franklin, M. K. (1990) 'Unchained', *Journal of Popular Film and Television*, 18, 3, 123–30.

Freedman, Estelle B. (1996) 'The Prison Lesbian: Race, Class and the Construction of the Aggressive Female Homosexual, 1915–1965', *Feminist Studies*, 22, 2, 397–423.

Gonthier, David Jr. (2006) *American Prison Films Since 1930: From The Big House to The Shawshank Redemption*. Lewiston, NY: Edwin Mellen Press.

Griffiths, Alison (2012) 'Bound by Cinematic Chains: Film and Prisons During the Early Era', in Andre Gaudreault, Nicolas Dulac and Santiago Hidalgo (eds) *A Companion to Early Cinema*. Malden: Wiley-Blackwell, 420–40.

Gutierrez, Peter (2013) 'Redeeming the Myth of Upward Mobility: *The Shawshank Redemption*', *Screen Education*, 70, 98–103.

Halliwell, Martin (2007) *American Culture in the 1950s*. Edinburgh: Edinburgh University Press.

Hall, Mordaunt (1930) 'A Jail-Break', *New York Times*, 25 June.

____ (1932) 'Life Ends'. *New York Times*, 26 August.

Hamilton, Emma and Troy Saxby (2011) '"Draggin' the Chain"': Linking Civil Rights and African American Representation in *The Defiant Ones* and *In the Heat of the Night*', *Black Camera*, 3, 1, 75–95.

Hanson, Philip (2008) *This Side of Despair: How the Movies and American Life Intersected During the Great Depression*. Madison, NJ: Fairleigh Dickinson University Press.

Hernan, Vera and Andrew M. Gordon (2003) *Screen Saviors: Hollywood Fictions of Whiteness*. Lanham, MD: Roman and Littlefield.

Hicks, Heather J. (2003) 'Hoodoo Economics: White Men's Work and Black

Men's Magic in Contemporary American Film', *Camera Obscura*, 53, 18, 2, 27–55.

Horton, Andrew (1984) 'Jules Dassin: A Multinational Filmmaker Considered', *Film Criticism*, 8, 3, 21–35.

Kaplan, E. Ann (1992) *Motherhood and Representation: The Mother in Popular Culture and Melodrama*. New York: Routledge.

Kimmel, Michael and Amy Aronson (2004) *Men and Masculinities: A Social, Cultural, and Historical Encyclopedia*. Vol. 1. Santa Barbara, CA: ABC-CLIO.

Kozloff, Sarah (2014a) 'Melodrama', in Lester Friedman, David Desser, Sarah Kozloff, Martha Nochimson and Stephen Prince (eds) *An Introduction to Film Genres*. New York: W. W. Norton, 80–117.

____ (2014b) 'The Social-Problem Film' in Lester Friedman, David Desser, Sarah Kozloff, Martha Nochimson and Stephen Prince (eds) *An Introduction to Film Genres*. New York: W. W. Norton, 446–481.

LaChance, Daniel (2015) 'White Masculinity and Harsh Punishment in 1990s Popular Culture', in Charles J. Ogletree, Jr. and Austin Sarat (eds) *Punishment in Popular Culture*. New York: New York University Press, 161–96.

Loader, Jayne (1985) 'Jeanne Dielman: Death in Installments', in Bill Nichols (ed.) *Movies and Methods: An Anthology*, Vol. 2. Berkeley, CA: University of California Press.

Marion, Frances (1972) *Off with Their Heads: A Serio-Comic Tale of Hollywood*. New York: Macmillian.

Mason, Paul (2006) 'Relocating Hollywood's Prison Film Discourse', in Paul Mason (ed.) *Captured by the Media: Prison Discourse in Popular Culture*. Cullompton: Willan Publishing, 191–209.

McCarthy, Todd (1997) *Howard Hawks: The Grey Fox of Hollywood*. New York: Grove Press.

Michel, Sonja (1999) *Children's Interests/Mother's Rights: The Shaping of America's Child Care Policy*. New Haven, CT: Yale University Press.

Morey, Anne (1995) '"The Judge Called Me an Accessory": Women's Prison Films, 1950–1962', *Journal of Popular Film and Television*, 23, 2, 80–7.

Morrison, Toni (1989) 'Unspeakable Things Unspoken: The Afro-American Presence in American Literature', *Michigan Quarterly Review*, 28, 1–34.

Munby, Jonathan (1999) *Public Enemies, Public Heroes: Screening the*

*Gangster Film from Little Caesar to Touch of Evil*. Chicago: University of Chicago Press.

Nadel, Alan (1995) *Containment Culture: American Narratives, Postmodernism, and the Atomic Age*. Durham, NC: Duke University Press.

Nero, Charles I. (2004) 'Diva Traffic and Male Bonding in Film: Teaching Opera, Learning Gender, Race, and Nation', *Camera Obscura*, 56, 19, 2, 47–73.

Osborne, Thomas Mott (1914) *Within Prison Walls: Being a Narrative of Personal Experience During a Week of Voluntary Confinement in the State Prison at Auburn, New York*. New York: D. Appelton.

____ (1916) *Society and Prisons: Some Suggestions for a New Penology*. New Haven, CT: Yale University Press.

Parker, James (2010) 'Prison Porn', *The Atlantic*, March; http://www.theatlantic.com/magazine/archive/2010/03/prison-porn/307906/

Prassel, Frank Richard (1993) *The Great American Outlaw: A Legacy of Fact and Fiction*. Norman, OK: University of Oklahoma Press.

Prince, Stephen (2014) 'The Western', in Lester Friedman, David Desser, Sarah Kozloff, Martha Nochimson and Stephen Prince (eds) *An Introduction to Film Genres*. New York: W. W. Norton, 242–77.

Rafter, Nicole (2006) *Shots in the Mirror: Crime Films and Society*. Oxford: Oxford University Press.

Roffman, Peter and Jim Purdy (1981) *The Hollywood Social Problem Film: Madness, Despair and Politics from the Depression to the Fifties*. Bloomington, IN: Indiana University Press.

Schatz, Thomas (2012) 'The Structural Influence: New Directions in Film Genre Study', in Barry Keith Grant (ed.) *Film Genre Reader IV*. Austin: University of Texas Press, 110–20.

Sontag, Susan (2008) 'Notes on Camp', in Ernest Mathijs and Xavier Mendik (eds) *The Cult Film Reader*. New York: Open University Press, 41–52.

Stein, Abby (2012) 'Back on the Chain Gang: The New/Old Prison Labor Paradigm', *The Journal of Psychohistory*, 39, 4, 254–60.

Verdeyen, Robert J. (1995) 'Correctional Industries: Making Inmate Work Productive', *Corrections Today*, 57, 5, 106, 108–10.

Wallace, Aurora (2015) 'Prison Narratives in Reality Television' in Charles J. Ogletree Jr. and Austin Sarat (eds) *Punishment in Popular Culture*. New York: New York University Press, 55–75.

Walsh, Andrea S. (1984) *Women's Film and Female Experience: 1940–1950*. New York: Praeger.

Warner, Jack L. (1964) *My First Hundred Years in Hollywood*. New York: Random House.

Whissel, Kristin (2015) 'The Spectacle of Punishment and the "Melodramatic Imagination" in the Classical-Era Prison Film: *I Am a Fugitive from a Chain Gang* (1932) and *Brute Force* (1947)', in Charles J. Ogletree, Jr. and Austin Sarat (eds) *Punishment in Popular Culture*. New York: New York University Press, 79–116.

Williams, Linda (2001) 'Melodrama in Black and White: Uncle Tom and *The Green Mile*', *Film Quarterly*, 55, 2, 14–21.

Williams, Linda Ruth and Michael Hammond (eds) (2006) *Contemporary American Cinema*. Maidenhead: Open University Press.

Wilson, David and Sean O'Sullivan (2004) *Images of Incarceration: Representations of Prison in Film and Television Drama*. Winchester: Waterside Press.

Wilson, Leslie Kreiner (2012) 'Frances Marion: Censorship and the Screenwriter in Hollywood, 1929–1931', *Journal of Screenwriting*, 3, 2, 131–55.

Wood, Robin (1986) *Hollywood from Vietnam to Reagan*. New York: Columbia University Press.

# INDEX

*20,000 Years in Sing Sing* 12, 17, 23

Abu Ghraib 106–8
*American History X* 91–2
*American Me* 88–9
anti-drug laws 101
antihero 77
*At the Death House Door* 105
*Attica* 100, 111

*Bad Girls* 4
Baldwin, James 74, 76–7
big house era 18, 20, 22
*Big House, The* 5, 11, 18, 23–4, 26–8, 30–1, 35–6, 38, 42
Blackface 29
boarding school movies 15
*Boys of Abu Ghraib* 107–8
*Broken on All Sides* 102
*Bronson* 8
*Brute Force* 86
buddy films 72, 75, 80–1
Bush, George W. 106, 108

*Caged* 30, 46–9, 51–5
Camp 48, 53
*Camp X-Ray* 108
capital punishment 100, 103, 105

Carter, Jimmy 2–4
chain gangs 11, 13, 18, 37–42, 75, 77, 103
Chaplin, Charlie 15
Cheney, Dick 106, 108
child care 58–62
Clinton, Bill 92, 97
Clocks 36
Coates, Ta-Nehisi 99
Cold War era 45
*Con Air* 93
*Condemned!* 5
contagion 49, 51
containment narratives 46
*Convict 13* 5
*Coogan's Bluff* 2
*Cool Hand Luke* 7
*Criminal Code, The* 23, 31–2, 35–7, 42

Darabont, Frank 92, 94
Davis, Angela Y. 110
*Dead Man Walking* 103
*Defiant Ones, The* 14, 16, 71–4, 76–7, 84
*Detained* 5
*Detour* 43
*Dirty Harry* 2–3
*Double Indemnity* 66

Dyer, Richard  69, 86

Each Dawn I Die  18, 29, 42
Eastwood, Clint  1–4, 87
echoes of incarceration  102
enemy combatants  98, 106
Escape from Alcatraz  1–3, 7, 86–7
Experimenter, The  99, 105

Face/Off  93
Family Man, The  94
Farm: 10 Down, The  103
Farm: Angola U.S.A., The  102–3
Federal Bureau of Prisons  22
femme fatale  60
Fistful of Dollars, A  2
Fog of War, The  106
For a Few Dollars More  2
Ford, John  28
Foucault, Michel  6
Frontline  106

gangster genre  9, 17–20
Garrett, P.W.  24
gas chamber  63, 66–7, 104–5
Get Hard  86
Ghosts of Abu Ghraib  107
Gibney, Alex  100, 108
Gilbert, Peter  105
Godless Girl, The  44
Good, the Bad and the Ugly, The  2
Grand Illusion  29
Green Mile, The  8, 16, 92–5, 97
Guantánamo Bay  106, 108, 111
Guantánamo: Blacked Out Bay  108

Hawes Cooper Act  27
Hays Office  24
Hell's Highway  23, 37–41
Herzog, Werner  5, 103–5
heterosexuality  51, 79, 85
Hill, George W.  5, 18, 24
homosexuality  49, 51, 57
homosocial bond  75–6

Hoose-Gow, The  5
House I Live In, The  100, 102
House of Women  46, 57–9, 61–2,
House Un-American Activities
   Committee  50
Hurricane, The  93

I Am a Fugitive from a Chain Gang
   11–13, 23, 38–42, 77
I Want to Live!  30, 46, 63–5, 67
Ice-T  97
Innocence Project, The  100
Innocent Man, An  11, 68, 70–1
Into the Abyss  103, 105
Irreversible  89

Jackson County Jail  89
Jailhouse Rock  11, 14
Jarecki, Eugene  100, 101
Johnny Holiday  88
juvenile hall  87, 88

Karloff, Boris  31–2
Keaton, Buster  5
Kellogg, Virginia  47
Kennedy, John F.  59
King, Rodney  97
Kinsey reports  45
Kiss of the Spider Woman  85
Kramer, Stanley  72–3

Ladies of the Big House  18, 23, 45
Lady and the Tramp  46–7
Last Mile, The  23, 32–3, 35–7, 42
Laurel and Hardy  5, 72
Lawes, Lewis  33
Legend of Bagger Vance, The  94
lesbianism  50–1
Lesson Before Dying, A  93
Life and Death Row  105
Little Caesar  18–19
Lockup  4
Longest Yard, The  12, 30, 80–2,
   84–85

madness 24, 31, 35, 54, 56
magical black man, the 94
mandatory minimum sentences 102
Marion, Frances 5, 24
martyrs 80
masculinity 19, 29, 72, 80, 84–6,
    88–9, 92, 94
mass incarceration 16, 93, 97,
    99–100, 102, 109, 111
*Mayor of Hell, The* 15, 23
McCarthy, Joseph 50
*Meet the Press* 108
Melodrama 5, 20, 36, 42–3, 48
mental institution movies 15
*Midnight Express* 7, 90
Milgram, Stanley 105
miscommunication 41–2
*Misery* 12, 15
*Modern Times* 15
Montgomery, Edward S. 63, 65–7, 73
Morris, Errol 100, 104, 106
Morrison, Toni 93
Mothers 36–7, 46, 49, 57–60, 62
*Mr. Death: The Rise and Fall of Fred A.
    Leuchter* 104

New Penology Movement, The 5,
    21–2
*Night Of, The* 7
*No Place Like Jail* 5
Nostalgia 94

Obama, Barack 111
*Orange is the New Black* 4
Osborne, Thomas Mott 21–2
*Oz* 4, 85

*Pardon Us* 5
penal eras 21
*Penitentiary* 84–5
*Pierrepoint: The Last Hangman* 104
Poitier, Sidney 14, 72–4, 84
Popular Front movement 20
pregnancy 56

*Prison Break* 4
prison-industrial complex 101–2
prison reality shows 5–6, 100
prisoner of war films 15
Progressive Era 21
Prostitution 51, 64
*Public Enemy, The* 18–19
Public Welfare Amendments 59

rape 51, 70–1, 84–92, 109
Reagan, Ronald 3
recidivism 102
Report on Penal Institutions,
    Probation and Parole, The 22
*Riot in Cellblock 11* 12
*Road to Guantánamo, The* 108
*Rock, The* 93
Rumsfeld, Donald 106

*Second Hundred Years, The* 5
Selleck, Tom 68
sequels 94
*Sex in Chains* 5
sexploitation 67
sexual inversion 49, 51
*Shawshank Redemption, The* 7, 71,
    86, 91, 92, 94–7
Siegel, Don 1–3
Simon, David 101
Simpson, O.J. 97
*Sin of Nora Moran, The* 45
Slavery 38, 40, 103
*Sleepers* 88
social problem film 20, 38, 43, 48,
    52, 89
sports 80–1, 84
*Standard Operating Procedure* 100,
    106–7
*Stanford Prison Experiment, The* 105
*Star Wars* 11
*Starred Up* 109–10
Steiner, Max 49
*Stir Crazy* 11, 84–5
Stone, Oliver 90

*Straw Dogs* 89
super-predators 97

*Taxi to the Dark Side* 100, 108
Thalberg, Irving 24
'Three Strikes' law 93
Tipton Three, The 108
Torture 6, 36, 38, 54, 66, 98, 105–7
*True Crime* 93
*Truman Show, The* 15
*Two Mules for Sister Sara* 2

*Unbreakable* 94
*Up the River* 23, 28–30, 36–7, 42

Van Waters, Miriam 52
Violent Crime Control and Law
    Enforcement Act 92

Warner, Jack 38
western genre 2, 10–12
*What Dreams May Come* 94
whiteness 69, 92
*Why Punish the Children?* 58,
*Why We Fight* 100
*Women's Prison* 44, 46, 53, 56–7

Zimbardo, Philip 106